ALL COLOUR HIGHWAY CODE

Question and Answer Quiz book

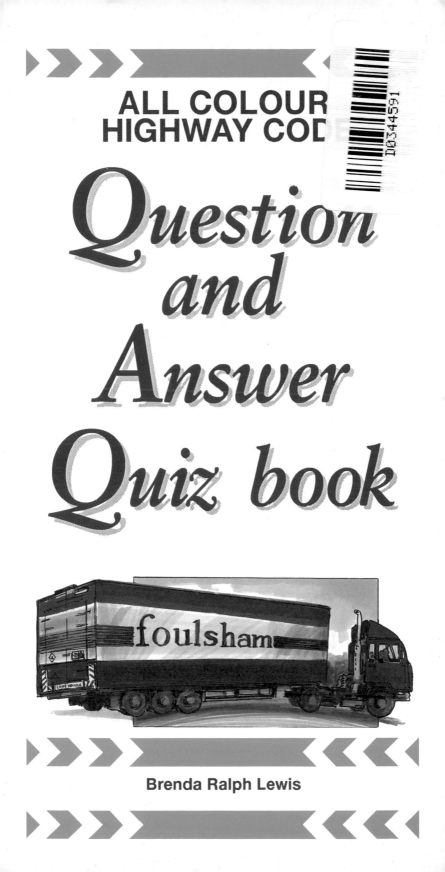

foulsham

Brenda Ralph Lewis

foulsham

Yeovil Road, Slough, Berkshire, SL1 4JH

The Author and Publisher gratefully acknowledge permission
by the Controller of Her Majesty's Stationery Office to
reproduce the signs from The Highway Code.

Printed in Great Britain
at The Westdale Press, Cardiff.

ALL COLOUR HIGHWAY CODE
Question and Answer Quiz book

The Highway Code is a handbook of good behaviour on the road and stresses above all, safety and consideration for others. It also has the force of law behind it and is an integral part of the exam which is The Driving Test. To many learner drivers that makes it daunting, even fearsome.

The All colour Highway Code Question and Answer Quiz Book

aims to take the fear out of the code by presenting it in a form more usually associated with entertainment. The whole of the code is here in Question and Answer form, covering every aspect of driving, cycling and walking on the road as well as the signs and signals that help road users navigate the roads safely. We hope you will find it stimulating, as quizzes are meant to be, but its purpose is no less serious than that of the code itself; to make you an alert and considerate road user, aware of the dangers and responsibilities of that status.

The All Colour Highway Code Question and Answer Quiz Book is divided into the sections found in the Highway Code itself and for ease of reference, question numbers are the same as the rule numbers in the original Department of Transport publication. If there's more than one question arising from a rule, they are indicated as A], B],and so on. Good quizzing - and safe road using!

*P*edestrians

GENERAL

1] *While on a pavement or footpath, you find you have to walk near the kerb. In this situation, should you face the oncoming traffic or have your back to it?*

2] *On a road with no pavement or footpath, do you walk*
i] on the left hand OR
ii] the right hand side of the road?

3] *Does oncoming traffic have a better chance of seeing you if you*
i] walk on the right of a sharp right hand bend in the road?
ii] walk on the left of the bend?
iii] walk in single file
iv] walk two or more abreast?
v] wear light-coloured, fluorescent or bright clothing?
vi] wear reflective clothing?

4] *Should very young children, say, under two years of age, be strapped into:*
i] push chairs
ii] reins
iii] or be held by the hand?

5A] *There is an organised march involving several people and animals [See also Rule 214] moving along a road.*
On which side of the road should they move?

5B] *Does the march need people acting as lookouts*
i] in front of the group
ii] at the back of the group wearing fluorescent clothes at night
iii] at both the front and back wearing reflective clothes at night
iv] at both the front and the back wearing fluorescent clothes in the daytime

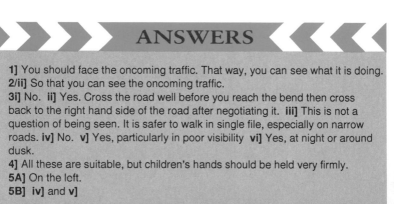

►►►► ANSWERS ◄◄◄◄

1] You should face the oncoming traffic. That way, you can see what it is doing.
2/ii] So that you can see the oncoming traffic.
3i] No. **ii]** Yes. Cross the road well before you reach the bend then cross back to the right hand side of the road after negotiating it. **iii]** This is not a question of being seen. It is safer to walk in single file, especially on narrow roads. **iv]** No. **v]** Yes, particularly in poor visibility **vi]** Yes, at night or around dusk.
4] All these are suitable, but children's hands should be held very firmly.
5A] On the left.
5B] **iv]** and **v]**

*P*edestrians

5C] *At night, what lights should be carried on the march:*
i] a bright red light in the front
ii] a white light at the back
iii] a white light at the front and a red light at the back
iv]a line of lights carried by people on the outside of the march
6:] SEE QUESTION ON RULE 155 [MOTORWAYS]

CROSSING THE ROAD

THE GREEN CROSS CODE HELPS PEDESTRIANS CROSS ROADS SAFELY.

7A] *At what age should children be able to use the Green Cross Code properly and how can parents and other adults make sure that they do?*

7B] *Which of these places are best for crossing the road and which should be avoided?*
i] Zebra, Pelican or Puffin crossings
ii] Traffic lights
iii] Islands in the middle of the road
iv] Footbridges
v] Where a traffic warden, police officer or school crossing patrol is on duty
vi] Subways
vii] Anywhere on the road as long as you can see clearly
viii] Between cars parked by the side of the road
ix]Level crossings

7C] *It is safe to cross the road if there is no traffic near, but what must you remember about traffic further off?*

►►►► ANSWERS ◄◄◄◄

5C] iii] The red light at the back should be bright, and visible from behind.
7A] It depends on the child, though young children should never be allowed out alone on the pavement or road. Parents must decide when a child understands the Code and can help by using it themselves.
7B] i] ii] iii] iv] v] vi] and **vii]**   are best. **viii]** Standing between parked cars means that oncoming traffic may not see you.**ix]** Level crossings are not road crossings, but places where rail lines cross the road.
7C] Traffic may **LOOK** far away, but can be travelling fast and reach you more quickly than you think. Keep on watching it, therefore.

*P*edestrians

7D] *When preparing to walk across a road [don't run], how do you see if traffic is near*
i] from a pavement?
ii] from a road?

ISLANDS IN THE MIDDLE OF THE ROAD/ROAD JUNCTIONS

7E] 8] 9] *How do you cross a road if there is*
i] an island in the middle of the road?
ii] a road junction nearby?

CROSSING AT A ZEBRA CROSSING

10] *Why is it dangerous to cross a Zebra crossing at the side, where there are zigzag lines painted on the road?*
11A] *What should you remember about traffic - and not just at Zebra crossings - when roads are slippery because of rain or ice?*
11B] *What are you saying to road traffic when you put one foot on a Zebra crossing?*
12] *What must you look and listen for while walking across a Zebra?*
13] SEE ANSWER TO QUESTIONS .7E /8 /9

CROSSING AT A PELICAN CROSSING

14A] *What do you find at Pelican crossings but not at Zebras?*
14B] *What does it mean when the green figure at a Pelican crossing begins to flash?*

ANSWERS

7D] I] from near, but not ON the kerb **II]** back from approaching traffic, but not so far back that you cannot see it.
ISLANDS IN THE MIDDLE OF THE ROAD/ROAD JUNCTIONS
7E] 8] 9] i]Treat the road as if it were two roads. Stop on the island before crossing the second "road." Treat a Zebra with a central island the same way.
" Watch for traffic turning the corner."
CROSSING AT A ZEBRA CROSSING
10] The zigzag lines mark the area where traffic is coming to a halt at Zebra crossings. It is therefore still moving.
11A] When roads are slippery, vehicles take longer to stop.
11B] You are saying that you wish to cross the Zebra. You should not do so, or push a pram or wheelchair across until the traffic has stopped.
12] Look both ways and listen for vehicles whose drivers may not have seen you.
CROSSING AT A PELICAN CROSSING
Traffic lights at Pelican crossings tell the traffic when to stop and a "standing" red figure does the same for pedestrians. Pedestrians can activate the lights by pressing a button on a box attached to them. When the "walking" green figure shows, cross the Pelican.
14A] A bleep or voice which tells blind or partially sighted pedestrians when they can cross.
14B] It warns that the traffic is about to move. If you are already on the crossing, you can get safely to the other side. The same applies to tramway crossings where you may still be crossing when the amber light warning of an approaching tram starts to flash.

*P*edestrians

RULES 15-20

15A] *Should the "staggered" crossing in the picture (**Fig. 1**) be treated as one crossing or two?*

15B]*Which of these three signals is found only at Pelican crossings and what does it indicate.*
   FIG. 2

CROSSING AT A PUFFIN CROSSING

16] *What is the difference between signals, both operated by pedestrians, at Puffin and Pelican crossings? How do they work?*

CROSSING AT TRAFFIC LIGHTS

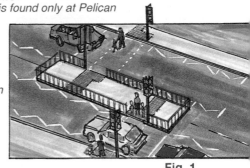

Fig. 1

17A] *What is the difference between the way the green "walking" figure operates at Pelicans and the way it operates at ordinary traffic lights?*

17B] *Sometimes, traffic lights enable vehicles in some lanes to move, while indicating to those in other lanes that they must stop. What does this mean for pedestrians?*

CROSSINGS CONTROLLED BY POLICE, TRAFFIC WARDENS OR SCHOOL CROSSING PATROLS

18] *Should you walk in front of or behind police officers, traffic wardens or school crossing patrols once they have signalled it is safe to cross the road?*

GUARD RAILS

19] *Where should you cross a road with guard rails?*

TACTILE PAVING
20] *What is the purpose of textured or tactile paving which pedestrians can "feel" with their feet?*

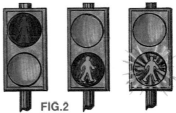

FIG.2

ANSWERS

15A] Two
15B] The third is found only at Pelicans and indicates that pedestrians should not start to cross. The two other signals are found at both Pelicans and some traffic lights.
CROSSING AT A PUFFIN CROSSING 16] At Puffins, the pedestrian signals are on the pedestrians' side of the road. Infra red detectors monitor them as they cross and control the time the red traffic light continues to show.
CROSSING AT TRAFFIC LIGHTS 17A] The"walking" figure does not flash at ordinary traffic lights. It just goes out.
17B] Pedestrians should stay alert for moving traffic and for vehicles turning a corner.
CROSSINGS CONTROLLED BY POLICE, TRAFFIC WARDENS OR SCHOOL CROSSING PATROLS 18] Cross in front so that you can be seen.
GUARD RAILS 19] Only at the gap in the rail which is there for the purpose. Never jump over the rails or walk between them and the traffic.
TACTILE PAVING 20] It enables blind or partially sighted pedestrians to "feel" where they should stand while waiting to cross a road.

*P*edestrians

CROSSING ONE WAY STREETS

21] *On one-way streets, most traffic moves in only one direction, but why should you look carefully at 'bus lanes which run along some one-way streets?*

CROSSING BUS AND CYCLE LANES

22] *What might buses do that is different from traffic in the road adjacent to a bus lane?*

22A] *Cyclists may use bus lanes or special cycle lanes, but what does a cycle lane usually look like?*

PARKED VEHICLES

23] *If a vehicle is parked where you wish to cross the road. where should you stand in relation to that vehicle?*

23A] *If a parked vehicle has its engine running, should you stand behind or in front of it?*

CROSSING THE ROAD AT NIGHT

24] *There is no pedestrian crossing or island at the place where you wish to cross the road at night. Where else can you cross the road safely? [See Also Question for Rule 3]*

EMERGENCY VEHICLES

25] *What should you do when police, ambulance or fire brigade emergency vehicles - heralded by sirens and flashing blue lights - are on the road near you? [See also Questions for Rules 76, 77 and 78]*

GETTING ON OR OFF A BUS

26A] *Should you get off a bus when it is slowing down to stop?*

26B] *After getting off, you want to cross the road. Should you cross behind or in front of the bus?*

 **ANSWERS**

CROSSING ONE WAY STREETS
   21] Bus lanes may contain buses moving in the opposite direction to the rest of the traffic.
CROSSING BUS AND CYCLE LANES
   22] Buses may be travelling faster, since their part of the road is often clearer.
   22A] A narrow strip by the kerb, just wide enough for cycle to pass.
PARKED VEHICLES
   23] On the outside edge of the car, a position from which you can look around to ensure you can see the traffic and the traffic can see you.
   23A] Neither behind nor in front. Keep well away from cars with their engines running. The driver may start up at any time.
CROSSING THE ROAD AT NIGHT
   24] At a street light, where drivers can see you more easily.
EMERGENCY VEHICLES
   25] Stay well away and off the road. Emergency vehicles are in a hurry and, in certain cases, someone's life may depend on them.
GETTING ON OR OFF A BUS 26A] Get off only when the bus has stopped.

Vehicles & Cyclists

RULES 27-30

RAILWAYS AND TRAMWAYS
27] *SEE RULE NO.225/234 AND 241/2]*

DRIVERS, MOTORCYCLISTS AND CYCLISTS
VEHICLE CONDITION

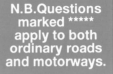

N.B.Questions marked ***** apply to both ordinary roads and motorways.

***** **28]** *Before driving on the road, your vehicle must be roadworthy. Of the features which must be in good order for this to be so — that is, clean **and** clear, or properly adjusted — which five have been omitted from this list: Tyres, exhaust system, lights, seat belts, demisters, windscreen wipers, windscreen, windows, reflectors, indicators, seat, head restraints, brakes.*

LOADS

***** **29]** Name two important factors in carrying loads safely on the roads.

MOTORCYCLES

***** **30A]** *TRUE OR FALSE?* When riding pillion on motorcycles, scooters or mopeds, you do not have to wear a helmet and eye protectors.

30B] *Why should you wear strong boots, gloves; and other protective clothing when riding a motorcycle*
i] To keep you warm
ii] To protect you if you fall off
iii] To protect your clothes against dirt and dust?

30C] When sitting astride on the passenger seat, where should you place your feet?

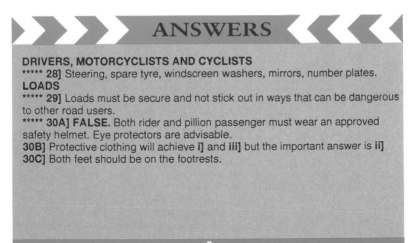

ANSWERS

DRIVERS, MOTORCYCLISTS AND CYCLISTS
***** **28]** Steering, spare tyre, windscreen washers, mirrors, number plates.
LOADS
***** **29]** Loads must be secure and not stick out in ways that can be dangerous to other road users.
***** **30A] FALSE.** Both rider and pillion passenger must wear an approved safety helmet. Eye protectors are advisable.
30B] Protective clothing will achieve **i]** and **iii]** but the important answer is **ii]**
30C] Both feet should be on the footrests.

30D] *What should motor cyclists and their passengers use or wear to be visible on the road?*
i] During the day.
ii] At night.
Dipped headlights, Reflective clothing, Fluorescent clothing, Light or brightly coloured clothing.

TIREDNESS OR ILLNESS

***** **31]** *You have had a late night or are starting a cold. Does it matter if you drive?*

***** **32]** *You feel tired or sleepy while driving. What should you do about it?*
i] Carry on, as the feeling will soon pass.
ii] Switch on your car radio or cassette/CD player.
iii] Stop somewhere safe and have a rest.
iv] Get some fresh air into your car.

***** **33]** *You have a headache and take a painkiller for it. Should you drive afterwards?*

VISION

***** **34]** *People who wear spectacles or contact lenses should not drive.* **TRUE OR FALSE?**

***** **35]** *Why are tinted features such as glasses, windows or windscreens a bad idea when driving at night or in poor visibility?*

LEARNERS

36] *When practising on the road, learner drivers have to be accompanied by someone able to supervise them. The supervisor's minimum age should be*
i] 18   **ii]** 25   **iii]** 21   **iv]**   28
and s/he should have held a current British license for
v] 5 years   **vi]** 1 year   **vii]** 2 years   **viii]** 3 years

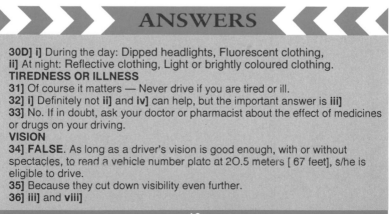

▶▶▶ ANSWERS ◀◀◀

30D] i] During the day: Dipped headlights, Fluorescent clothing,
ii] At night: Reflective clothing, Light or brightly coloured clothing.
TIREDNESS OR ILLNESS
31] Of course it matters — Never drive if you are tired or ill.
32] i] Definitely not **ii]** and **iv]** can help, but the important answer is **iii]**
33] No. If in doubt, ask your doctor or pharmacist about the effect of medicines or drugs on your driving.
VISION
34] FALSE. As long as a driver's vision is good enough, with or without spectacles, to read a vehicle number plate at 20.5 meters [67 feet], s/he is eligible to drive.
35] Because they cut down visibility even further.
36] iii] and **viii]**

*D*riving

37] *While learning [with an approved training company] how to ride a motorcycle, scooter or moped, which of the following are you allowed to do?*
i] pull a trailer
ii] carry passengers
iii] on your own, ride a motorcycle of 900 cc engine capacity or
iv] of 125cc engine capacity or
v] 550 cc engine capacity?

38] Cars used by learner drivers must carry L plates at all times. **TRUE OR FALSE?**

ALCOHOL AND THE MOTORIST

***** 39A]** *You have a blood alcohol level of 100 mgs. in 100 millilitres of blood after drinking, say, more than two pints of ordinary strength bitter. Are you fit to drive?*

39B] TRUE OR FALSE? *Even if you have a blood alcohol level above the legal limit, you can drive as long as your reactions, co ordination and judgement are unaffected.*

SEAT BELTS

***** 40]** and **41]** *Failing an appropriate child restraint [the best choice] which of these young passengers can wear an adult seat belt?*
i] a child aged 12 or 13 years
ii] a child under 13, but 1.5 meters [about 5 feet] in height
iii] A child under 3 years of age
iv] A child 3 to 11 years, under 1.5 meters in height

CHILDREN IN CARS

***** 42A]** *Where should children sit when in the rear of*
i] an estate car
ii] a family saloon car
iii] a hatchback
iv] a sports car
v] a van

►►►► ANSWERS ◄◄◄◄

37] iv] A 125 cc engine capacity is the maximum for learner motorcyclists. The rest are not allowed.
38] FALSE. L-plates need to be attached to private vehicles only when a learner driver is in control of it. Otherwise, plates should be removed or covered up.
ALCOHOL AND THE MOTORIST
39A] No. Blood alcohol level should be no higher than 80 mgs. in 100 millilitres of blood to come within the legal limit.
39B] FALSE. Although alcohol affects different people in different ways. The limit stands in all cases.
SEAT BELTS
40] and **41] i] ii]** and **iv] iii]** Children under three **MUST** wear a child restraint i.e. baby carrier, child seat, harness or booster seat **[See Rule 41]**
CHILDREN IN CARS
42A] In all cases children must sit in the rear seats, not in the space behind them.

Driving

42B] *Where children are wearing seat belts and, therefore, cannot move around too freely, do you need to bother with safety locks on the doors?*

CAR TELEPHONES AND MICROPHONES
***** **43A]** *What is the great potential danger in using telephones or microphones while driving?*
43B] *While driving, which of the following can you use:*
i] a hands-free microphone
ii] a hand-held telephone
iii] a hand-held microphone
iv] a hands-free telephone

TRAFFIC SIGNALS AND TRAFFIC SIGNS
***** **44]** *Signals on the road include road markings, traffic lights and what else?*
45] 46] 47]: *Police officers [*****] traffic wardens and school crossing patrols [who must be obeyed] give signals to help warn or inform other road users. Which other road-users do, too?*

DRIVING YOUR VEHICLE — MOVING OFF
***** **48]** *What actions must you take before moving off?*

DRIVING ALONG
***** **49A]** *When can you drive on the right rather than the left?*
49B] *If someone wants to overtake you, do you*
i] Drop back and make a gap for the overtaking driver?
ii] Move up closer to the car in front
iii] Stay where you are?　　**[See also Rule 57]**
50] *When can you drive on a pavement or footpath?*

>>> ANSWERS <<<

42B] Yes.
CAR TELEPHONES AND MICROPHONES
43A] That you will lose control of your car because your hands and your attention are otherwise engaged.
43B] i] and **iv]** No, but permissible as long as it does not take your attention off the road. **ii]** No. **iii]** No. If you want to use your telephone/microphone, stop in a safe place first, though not on the hard shoulder of a motorway except in an emergency.
TRAFFIC LIGHT SIGNALS AND TRAFFIC SIGNS
44] Traffic signs sited by the roadside.
45] 46] 47] Drivers. You can use light indicators and hand signals to help and warn pedestrians and other road users.
DRIVING YOUR VEHICLE MOVING OFF
48] Look in your mirror, signal, if necessary, and look round for a final check.
DRIVING ALONG
49A] When overtaking, turning right, passing parked vehicles or driving past pedestrians in the road: in all cases, do so only as long as it is safe.
49B] i]
50] Only if you want to get into the driveway of a house or other property.

Driving

***** 51] *Before overtaking, why should you*
i] use your mirror
ii] signal?

52] *What characteristic of motorcycles and bicycles could pose a problem on the road, and what should drivers do when either of them is near [especially the drivers of long vehicles towing trailers]?*

53] *You are on a narrow, winding country road, driving a large slow moving vehicle. What should you do if traffic builds up behind you?*

SPEED LIMITS

54] *What speed per hour do street signs most often indicate?*

55] *In residential areas, you may find the road narrows, or there is a hump across the road, or a 20 mph speed limit sign is shown. What is their purpose?*

***** 56] *Where there is a speed limit, can you always drive up to that speed?*

STOPPING DISTANCES

***** 57A] *There is very heavy traffic on the road and vehicles are driving close to one another. Why is this potentially dangerous?*

2 SECONDS

57B] *When good conditions prevail, a two second gap between your car and the car in front may be sufficient. What gap should you leave if the roads are wet or icy?*

ANSWERS

51] To check whether other road users are behind or near you or on either side of your car, and to warn them that you are going to overtake.
52] Motorcycles and bicycles are narrower than other vehicles and more difficult to see. Give them plenty of room.
53] Move over into a safe place and let the traffic pass.
SPEED LIMITS
54] 30 mph, though there may be other signs showing other limits.
55] To slow traffic down and make the road safer for residents.
56] Not always, A speed limit is an indication. You have to take conditions on the road into account - whether it is wet, foggy or dark, and whether there are cyclists and pedestrians about.
STOPPING DISTANCES
57A] Because there may be too little space and time for vehicles to stop safely.
57B] A gap of four seconds on wet roads, but more when it is icy.

57C] *The faster you drive, the more stopping distance and time you need. What is the shortest stopping [that is thinking plus braking] distance when you are driving at:*
i] 60 mph
ii] 20 mph
iii] 40 mph
iv] 30 mph
v] 50 mph

57D] *At what speed are you driving if you need*
i] 18 meters [60 feet] thinking distance?
ii] 24 meters [180 feet] braking distance?
iii] 36 meters [120 feet] overall stopping distance?
iv] How many car lengths [average four meters each] do you need for the proper braking distance when driving at 70 mph?

FOG CODE

***** 58A] *When driving in fog, you need fog lights and*
i] dipped or
ii] full headlights?

58B] *At what speed should you drive in fog and how far should you be from the car in front?*

58C] *How can you tell if you are too close to the car in front when driving in fog?*

58D] *You see **FOG** on a lighted roadside sign, but there is no sign of fog on that part of the road. Do you presume that:*
i] Someone forgot to switch the sign off?
ii] There is fog up ahead
iii] The fog is patchy ?
iv] The sign is malfunctioning?

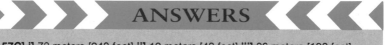

ANSWERS

57C] i] 73 meters [240 feet] **ii]** 12 meters [40 feet] **iii]** 36 meters [120 feet]
iv] 23 meters [75 feet] **v]** 53 metres [175 feet]
57D] i] 60 mph **ii]** 40 mph **iii]** 40 mph **iv]** 12.5 car lengths.

FOG CODE
58A] i] Dipped. Full headlights tend to bounce back off the fog.
58B] You should drive at a safe speed, slower than in normal conditions and at a distance from the car in front at which you can see clearly so as to pull up safely, if need be.
58C] When you can see the car in front, as opposed to its lights glowing through the gloom - except, that is, at very slow speeds.
58D] ii] and/or **iii]**

Driving

RULES 59-70

WINTER DRIVING

***** **59]** *For winter driving, which parts of your car need anti-freeze?*
i] Windscreen washer
ii] Battery
iii] Oil supply
iv] Radiator
v] Carburettor

***** **60A]** *If a road has been gritted to counteract freezing weather, can you drive as in normal dry conditions?*

60B] *Why do you need to take extra care, especially while riding a motorcycle, when overtaking a gritting lorry?*

***** **61]** *When driving in snow - do not do so unless it is essential - why is it important to use a high gear, avoid sudden acceleration or braking and not turn the steering wheel too fast?*

***** **62]** *There is a snow plough ahead. You want to overtake, but the plough is still clearing snow from the lane you mean to use. Should you overtake or wait?*

THE SAFETY OF PEDESTRIANS

63 — 70A inclusive] *You are driving through a crowded street in a residential area. What does it mean if you see;*
i] Someone carrying a white stick with two red reflective bands on it?
ii] An ice cream van parked by the side of the road
iii] A school warning sign with a flashing amber signal
iv] A **STOP — CHILDREN** sign.
v] A guide dog.
vi] A line of parked vehicles.

ANSWERS

WINTER DRIVING
59] I] and **iv]** but also make sure that the battery **[ii]** is in good order.
60A] No. An icy road can still be slippery despite the gritting.
60B] Because the lorry could be shooting out grit in your direction.
61] Any of these can cause your car to slide. Using a high gear cuts down the risk of wheel spin.
62] Wait. Snow ploughs throw out snow on both sides. Overtake only in a lane which has already been cleared.
THE SAFETY OF PEDESTRIANS
63 — 70A inclusive] i] The person is both blind and deaf and you need to give them plenty of time to cross the road. **ii]** There could be children about. They may not pay much attention to traffic with ice cream in mind. **iii]** Schoolchildren could be crossing the road ahead. **iv]** Displayed by a school crossing patrol, this sign means you must stop to let children across the road. **v]** The dog is leading a blind person, who will be carrying a white stick. **vi]** Pedestrians may suddenly emerge into the road from between parked cars.

Driving

70B] *What should you do if*
i] At a corner, you see pedestrians crossing the road into which you wish to turn or
ii] Pedestrians on a pavement you need to cross to enter a driveway or
iii] Pedestrians walking along narrow country roads with no pavement?

PEDESTRIAN CROSSINGS

71] *You are approaching a Zebra crossing. Pedestrians are waiting to cross, but none has yet stepped onto the Zebra. Do you drive on or stop?*

72-75 inclusive] YES or NO: *Can you*
i] Overtake at the zig-zag lines indicating a Zebra crossing or Pelican crossing?
ii] Overtake where there are no approach zig-zags?
iii] Drive on over a Pelican crossing with an island in the middle as long as your half of the crossing is clear?
iv] Hurry up pedestrians by flashing your lights or revving your engine?

▶▶▶ ANSWERS ◀◀◀

70B] In all cases, give way and allow pedestrians plenty of time and room.

PEDESTRIAN CROSSINGS

71] You stop.
72] — 75] incl.
i] No
ii] No
iii] No. Pedestrians may still be on the crossing.
but cross if the other half of the crossing is also clear.
iv] Never!

Driving

EMERGENCY VEHICLES/FLASHING AMBER LIGHTS

***** 76 — 78A incl.] *Each vehicle listed here may flash signals in a colour [shown (right). Match them up:*
i] Police car
ii] Ambulance
iii] Gritting lorry
iv] Tractor or other slow moving vehicle
v] Doctor's car
vi] Fire engine. **[See also question for rule 25]**

76/78B] *Which of these vehicles may also sound a siren?*

BUSES

79] You give way to a bus signalling that it is about to pull away from a bus stop, but what else must you look out for?

ANIMALS

80] *There are animals moving slowly on the road. Should you :*
i] Sound your horn or rev your engine to hurry them up.
ii] Drive quickly past them.
iii] Wait or drive slowly.

81] How do you know if a horserider, often a child, wishes to turn right?
i] When the horse moves to the centre of the road?
ii] When the rider signals ?
iii] When the rider looks behind to check the traffic?

SINGLE TRACK ROADS

82A] What is a single track road?
82B] What is a passing place and can you park there?
82C] *You are driving uphill on a single track road. Can you expect vehicles coming from the opposite direction to give way to you, or do you give way to them?*

►►►► ANSWERS ◄◄◄◄

EMERGENCY VEHICLES/FLASHING AMBER LIGHTS
76-78 incl.] i],ii],vi] Blue, iii] iv] Amber, v] A green signal indicates a doctor's car answering an emergency.
76 78B] i] ii] and vi]. They are all emergency vehicles. Police vehicles may also flash their headlights if they wish you to stop **[See Rule 78]** You must do so, pulling over to the side of the road when it is safe, and switching off your engine.
BUSES 79] Pedestrians crossing the road after getting off the bus.
ANIMALS 80] i] and ii] No. You could scare the animals and cause an accident. iii] is the correct answer.
81] ii] is safest. Horseriders may not move to the centre of the road i] before turning right iii] is not a certain indication.
SINGLE TRACK ROADS 82A] A road, often in a country area, where there is room for only one vehicle to drive.
82B] A passing place is a small bay on the left hand side of the road, where you pull in to let another vehicle pass. You must not park there.
82C] Vehicles from the opposite direction give way to you.

Driving

LINES AND LANES ALONG THE ROAD

*****83 — 87A incl. [87] _Match up the road markings in the first column with the procedure you should follow in the second:_

i] Double white lines, the line nearest to you broken.

ii] White diagonal strips painted on the road bordered by: an unbroken white line **or** a broken white line.

iii] Single white line with short gaps along the centre of the road.

iv] Short broken lines along the road.

v] Double white lines with line nearest to you unbroken.

vi] White chevrons painted on the road, bordered by an unbroken white line **or** a broken white line.

a] Do not cross or drive along the line unless moving out of a driveway, turning into a side road or getting round something stationary blocking your lane. **[RULE 84]**

b] Lines indicate driving lanes.

c] Strips or chevrons are there to separate traffic turning right: they mean either "Do not cross except in an emergency" or "Cross only when safe".

d] A hazard warning line. Do not cross unless the road ahead is clear **[RULE 83]**

e] You may cross the line to overtake when safe, as long as the line continues broken before you get back into lane. **[RULE 85]**

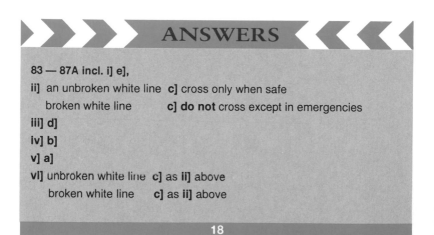

ANSWERS

83 — 87A incl. i] e],

ii] an unbroken white line **c]** cross only when safe
  broken white line **c] do not** cross except in emergencies

iii] d]

iv] b]

v] a]

vi] unbroken white line **c]** as **ii]** above
  broken white line **c]** as **ii]** above

Driving

87B] *Where will you find these coloured reflecting studs, together with white lines on the roadway?*
White studs
Amber studs
Green studs
Red studs

THE STUDS MARK:
i] Lanes in the road
ii] The left hand edge of the road
iii]The middle of the road
iv] The central reservation of a dual carriageway
v] Side roads
vi] A lay-by

88] *What is a crawler lane and which vehicles can use it?*

***** **89]** *What is lane discipline?*

***** **90]** *You are approaching a junction where the lanes go in different directions. How can you ensure you get into the right lane BEFORE reaching the junction?*

***** **91]** *You are in a traffic hold-up. What should you do?*
i] Move into another lane
ii] Move into another lane to get further ahead in your original lane?
iii] Turn into a side road on the left, hoping to find a clearer route to your destination.
iv] Stay where you are

***** **92] 94]***** 95A]** *What is the purpose of*
i] The middle lane on a three-lane single or dual carriageway
ii] The right-hand lane of a two-lane dual carriageway

93] SEE QUESTION TO RULE 93, [SEE PAGE 20]
95B] On a three lane dual carriageway, you have used
i] the middle lane or
ii] The right hand lane to overtake slower vehicles. What do you do next?

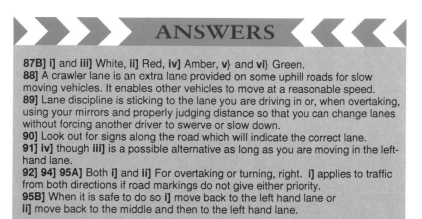

ANSWERS

87B] i] and iii] White, ii] Red, iv] Amber, v} and vi} Green.
88] A crawler lane is an extra lane provided on some uphill roads for slow moving vehicles. It enables other vehicles to move at a reasonable speed.
89] Lane discipline is sticking to the lane you are driving in or, when overtaking, using your mirrors and properly judging distance so that you can change lanes without forcing another driver to swerve or slow down.
90] Look out for signs along the road which will indicate the correct lane.
91] iv] though iii] is a possible alternative as long as you are moving in the left-hand lane.
92] 94] 95A] Both i] and ii] For overtaking or turning, right. i] applies to traffic from both directions if road markings do not give either priority.
95B] When it is safe to do so i] move back to the left hand lane or
ii] move back to the middle and then to the left hand lane.

Driving

93] *When can you use the right hand lanes on a single carriageway with four or more lanes?*

96A] *In a one-way street, which lane should you choose for*
i] driving straight on **ii]** turning left **iii]** turning right?

96B] *Traffic in one way streets obviously moves in one direction only, but what other feature is present that is not found on ordinary [two-way] roads?*

97] *When are you allowed to drive on special bus or tram lanes?*

98] *What is the difference between a cycle lane marked by* **i]** an unbroken white line and **ii]** a broken, white line?*

OVERTAKING

99] *You are about to overtake the car in front. You check the road behind to see that it is clear, move closer to the car in front, signal, then move out.*
i] What has been left out here ?
ii] Which procedure is wrong?

100] What is "cutting in" after overtaking?

101] *How much room should you allow when overtaking*
i] motorcyclists **ii]** pedal cyclists
   iii] horseriders
a] Less room than a car?
b] More room?
c] The same amount of room?

102-103] *When can you overtake on the left?*
i] When the vehicle in front is signalling a right turn
ii] On a three lane road when the lane in front of you is clear and there is a car travelling at normal speed in the middle lane ahead of you
iii] When there is a slow-moving queue of traffic on your right
iv] When you are "stuck" in a line of slow-moving traffic and want to get ahead?

ANSWERS

93] Only when road signs or markings say you can. Otherwise, keep to the left.
96A] i] The most appropriate, usually the clearest, lane. **ii]** The left hand lane unless signs indicate No Left Turn or other prohibition. **iii]** The right hand lane unless signs indicate No Right Turn or other prohibition.
96B] On one way streets, traffic can pass on either side of you at any point along their length.
97] Only outside the period in which they are operating, or when road markings or signs indicate you can use them at any time.
98] You must not drive or park on **i]** during its period of operation. Driving on **ii]** is allowed only when unavoidable.
OVERTAKING 99] i] You must check the road **AHEAD** as well as behind to see that it is clear **ii]** Moving **CLOSER** to the car in front is dangerous and obscures your view of the road ahead. Stay back.
100] Moving back into the left hand lane too close to the front of the car you have just overtaken or swerving into the left hand lane immediately ahead of another car instead of gliding gradually into it.
101] In all cases, the same amount of room as a car.
102-103] i] Yes, but only when it is safe. **ii]** No. **iii]** Yes . **iv]** No, though you can move into the left hand lane in order to turn left further on.

Driving

RULES 104-106

104] *When being overtaken should you*
i] Maintain your speed
ii] Drop back
iii] Increase your speed?

105] *On a two-lane single carriageway, vehicles are coming from the opposite direction just as you want to move out to get round vehicles or other obstacles parked in your lane. Do you overtake the obstacles or wait?*

106] *Can you overtake or not when*
i] Another vehicle is near, coming in the opposite direction?
ii] You are approaching a bridge?
iii] At a corner or right hand bend in the road?
iv] At a left hand bend in the road?
v] You are approaching a hump-backed bridge?
vi] You see the sign cancelling a No Overtaking restriction further back?
vii] On a hill
viii] On the brow of a hill
ix] On a level crossing
x] Approaching road junctions
xi] Along a bus or tram or cycle lane
xii] At road works
xiii] Where traffic is queueing at road junctions or road works
xiv] When you see a school crossing patrol
xv] Approaching a pedestrian crossing, but still in the zig-zag area
xvi] Over diagonal stripes or chevrons painted on the road or double white lines with the line nearer to you unbroken
xvii] Where the road narrows
xviii] By a stop being used by a bus or tram?

▶▶▶▶ ANSWERS ◀◀◀◀

104] i] Yes, unless it is necessary to slow down to let the vehicle overtaking you pass and pull in safely. **ii]** Yes **iii]** No.

105] Wait until the traffic from the opposite direction has moved past, then overtake.

106] i] No. The other vehicle may have to swerve or slow down to avoid you. **ii]** Yes, if safe. **iii]** No. **iv]** No. You must not overtake on ANY bend in the road. **v]** No. **vi]** No. You must wait until you have actually **passed** the cancelling sign. **vii]** Yes, if safe. **viii]** No. As with **iii] iv]** and **v]** you cannot see far enough ahead to know that it is safe. **ix]** No. **x]** No. **xi]** No. **xii]** Yes, if safe **xiii]** No **xiv]** No **xv]** No. **xvi]** No. **xvii]** No **xviii]** Yes, but not if it means driving between the bus or tram and the kerb.

*R*oad *J*unctions

RULES 107-110

ROAD JUNCTIONS

107] *Why should you take special care when approaching long vehicles making a turn at a junction?*

108] *Should you allow pedestrians to cross the road at a junction, or do you expect them to wait until you turn the corner?*

109] *There is an unbroken line across road at a junction. What else can you expect to see?*

110] *What type of white line could you find across the road when you see*
i] GIVE WAY sign?
ii] Where will the sign be?
iii] What alternative sign might you find?

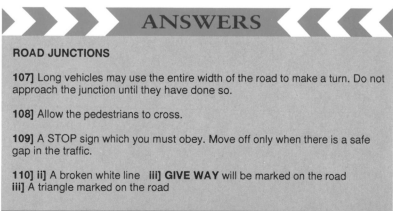

ANSWERS

ROAD JUNCTIONS

107] Long vehicles may use the entire width of the road to make a turn. Do not approach the junction until they have done so.

108] Allow the pedestrians to cross.

109] A STOP sign which you must obey. Move off only when there is a safe gap in the traffic.

110] ii] A broken white line   **iii] GIVE WAY** will be marked on the road
iii] A triangle marked on the road

Road Junctions

111] *While waiting at a junction to turn left, you see a vehicle approaching from your right, signalling its own left turn. You therefore go ahead and turn left. Where could you have gone wrong?*

112] *When going across a dual carriageway or turning right into it [See Rule 120] you may have to do so in two goes, pausing in the central reservation for a safe gap in the traffic before completing your maneuver. Under what circumstances can you NOT do this and what should you do instead?*

113A] *What colour and type of lines are painted on the road at box junctions?*

113B] *Normally, you should wait until your exit lane from a box junction Is clear, and you can drive straight across. What is the exception to this rule?*

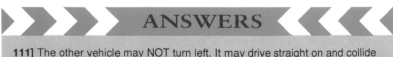

ANSWERS

111] The other vehicle may NOT turn left. It may drive straight on and collide with yours. Wait until it actually turns left, then move out.

112] When your vehicle is too large to fit safely into the length of the reservation, wait until the traffic is clear enough for you to drive straight across or turn right in one go, without pausing.

113A] Yellow criss-cross lines

113B] When oncoming traffic or traffic waiting to turn right impedes your own right turn.

Road Junctions

JUNCTIONS CONTROLLED BY TRAFFIC LIGHTS

114] *You have halted at the white **STOP** line across your side of a road at a junction, waiting for the lights to turn green. The lights turn green, but you find you cannot drive on. Why not?*

115] *What is indicated by a green arrow attached to some traffic lights?*

116] *If the traffic lights have failed, how should you proceed?*

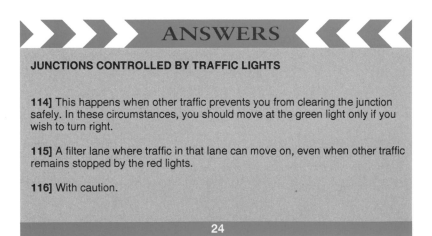

ANSWERS

JUNCTIONS CONTROLLED BY TRAFFIC LIGHTS

114] This happens when other traffic prevents you from clearing the junction safely. In these circumstances, you should move at the green light only if you wish to turn right.

115] A filter lane where traffic in that lane can move on, even when other traffic remains stopped by the red lights.

116] With caution.

Road Junctions

TURNING RIGHT

117A] *Put these procedures for turning right into the correct order:*
i] Drive into position for turning right in the centre of the road or a specially marked, space.
ii] Check for cyclists, motorcyclists and pedestrians.
iii] Signal your right turn.
iv] Check the traffic behind you using your mirrors.
v] Wait for a safe gap in traffic coming towards you before you make a right turn.

117B] *When it comes to checking the traffic, what is the difference between a main road and turning right off it?*

118] 119] *Another vehicle wants to turn right at a junction at the same time as you. As long as there is sufficient room, how should you and the other driver position yourselves.*
i] Nearside to nearside
ii] Nearside to offside
iii] Offside to offside
iv] Or should one of you hold back until the other has completed the right turn?

120] SEE QUESTION TO RULE 112]

ANSWERS

117A] **iv] iii] i] v] ii]**

117B] When turning right into a main road, you have to keep an eye on traffic moving in **BOTH** directions, not just your own, in order to know when there is a safe gap.

118] 119] iii] Offside to offside means you keep the other car on your right and turn behind it. If the junction is not suitable for offside to offside turning, nearside to nearside turning **i]** is permitted as long as both drivers have a good view of oncoming traffic **ii]** is not correct **iv]** is not usually necessary.

Signals

RULES 121-128

TURNING LEFT

121] 122] *Preparing to turn left, you have already checked traffic behind you and given the left turn signal. There is a motorcyclist on your right and, diagonally across the junction where you want to turn left, a bus is using a bus lane. The bus is about to drive across the side road into which you wish to turn.* **When do you turn left?**

ROUNDABOUTS

123A] *How should you prepare to use a roundabout before actually reaching it?*

123B] *At roundabouts, you should give way to traffic on your right, except ....* **WHEN?**

123C] *There are two roundabouts at a junction. How do you proceed?*

124] *When driving on a roundabout how do you signal when* **YOU WANT TO**

i] Go straight on
ii] Turn right off the roundabout
iii] Turn left off the roundabout
iv] Go right round.

> **DO YOU...** **a]** Signal left   **b]** Signal left, then right
> **c]** Signal right, then left   **d]** Signal right
> **e]** Not signal at all [There can be more than one answer]

125] *When will you find vehicles crossing in front of you while driving on a roundabout?*

126] *Where will you often find motorcyclists, cyclists and horseriders on a roundabout?*

127]128] *What do you do if you see long vehicles on or approaching a roundabout or mini-roundabout?*

▶▶▶ ANSWERS ◀◀◀

TURNING LEFT
121]122] Only after the motorcyclist and the bus have both moved on.

ROUNDABOUTS
123A] Look at the road signs to choose which exit off the roundabout you wish to take and reduce your speed.

123B] When road markings indicate otherwise.

123C] You treat them as two roundabouts and follow the roundabout rules at each one.

124] **i] e]** Do not signal on approaching the roundabout, then, **a]** Signal left after passing the exit before the one you wish to take. **ii] c]** Signal right then signal left after passing the exit before the one you wish to take.
iii] a] **iv]** as **ii]** above

125] Usually when they want to leave by the next exit.

126] Normally, they keep to the left, but may signal right if they intend to continue around the roundabout.

127]128] Because of their size, long vehicles may not follow the same roundabout rules as smaller vehicles. For instance, on mini-roundabouts, long vehicles may drive straight across the centre.

Signals

REVERSING

129] *When reversing, you must make sure that nothing is behind you - no other vehicles, obstructions or pedestrians, especially children. But what do you do about the "blind spot" behind your car where you cannot see?*

130] *Can you reverse*
i] Into a major road from a side street?
ii] Into a side street from a main road?
iii] From the road into a driveway?
iv] Out of a driveway into the road?

VEHICLE LIGHTS AND FOG LIGHTS

131A] *All your lights are clean and in good working order, but what can happen if the headlights are not properly adjusted as well?*
**** 131B]132]133] *Your car has* sidelights, full or dipped headlights, fog lights.
Which of these do you use in the following situations:
i] Seriously reduced visibility.
ii] When you cannot see more than 100 meters [328 feet] ahead.
iii] On unlit roads.
iv] Between sunset and sunrise.
v] On roads where street lights are more than 185 meters [600 feet] apart and a 30 mph speed limit is in force.
vi] Between half an hour after sunset and half an hour before sunrise.
vii] At night on motorways which are lit.
viii] When approaching vehicles at night, either from behind or coming in the opposite direction.
ix] At night in built up areas that are not well lit.
x] During the day when the sky is very overcast.

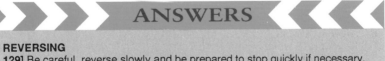

ANSWERS

REVERSING
129] Be careful, reverse slowly and be prepared to stop quickly if necessary. Do not drive in reverse for longer than you have to.
130] i] No. **ii]** and **iii]** Yes, but carefully **iv]** No. It is better to reverse in and drive out.
VEHICLE LIGHTS AND FOG LIGHTS
131A] Badly adjusted headlights can dazzle others on the road at night and cause accidents.
131B]132]133]
i] ii] full or dipped headlights, or front fog lights.
iii] iv] v] vi] vii] full or dipped headlights.
viii] dipped headlights, so as not to dazzle other drivers.
ix] dipped.
x] dipped or dim-dipped if your car has this feature.

Driving RULES 134-138

HAZARD WARNING LIGHTS

**** 134] *Can you use your hazard warning lights while driving*
i] on a motorway
ii] on ordinary roads
iii] on an unrestricted dual carriageway?

FLASHING HEADLIGHTS/ USE OF HORN

**** 135]136A] *When other drivers flash headlights or sound the car horn at you, does it mean:*
i] They want you to stop so as to turn in front of you.
ii] They are going to stop so that you can drive on.
iii] They are going to park, so please allow room.
iv] They want you to notice them.
v] They want to thank you for giving way?

136B] *Can you use your car horn*
i] At midnight
ii] at 0645 hours
iii] when stationary
iv] when a moving vehicle endangers your stationary car?

WAITING AND PARKING

137] When parking by the side of a street, how can other road or pavement users to be inconvenienced [unless you take care] **WHEN:**
i] You park close to a car displaying a "disabled" badge
ii] You open the driver's door to get out
iii] Your passengers get out into the road
iv] You forget to put the handbrake on
v] Your passengers get out onto the pavement?

**** 138] Can you pick up or set, down passengers by stopping or parking on a road marked with double lines, one of which is broken?

ANSWERS

HAZARD WARNING LIGHTS
134] i] and **iii]** Yes, but only to warn other drivers of obstructions or hazards ahead **ii]** No. You can use hazard warning lights only when you have stopped to warn other drivers that your car represents a temporary obstruction.
FLASHING HEADLIGHTS/USE OF HORN
135]136A] iv] The only valid reason for flashing headlights or sounding horns is to tell other drivers of your presence.
136B] i] No **ii]** No [do not use your car horn between 2330 and 0700 hours] **iii]** No **iv]** Yes
WAITING AND PARKING
137] i] You may leave too little room for the disabled driver
ii] Other road users may be hit or have to swerve unless you watch out for them first. **iii]** They should not get out into the road, but onto the pavement.
iv] Your car may move and collide with adjacent vehicles
v] Other pavement users could be hit or forced to step out of the way.
138] Yes, but not for any other reason. *[NB. Rest of provisions under Rule 138 are dealt with elsewhere.]*

Driving RULES 139-144

139A] *Where parking restrictions are in force between certain times, where will you find the signs indicating those times?*

139B]140]141] *Can you park*
i] Near a bus stop or school entrance
ii] 15 meters [49 feet] from a junction
iii] In front of an entrance or a place where the kerb has been lowered for wheelchair users
iv] On a pavement or footpath
v] Near a taxi rank, the brow of a hill, a hump-backed bridge or a level crossing
vi] 8 meters [26 feet] from a junction in an authorised parking space
vii] Opposite a traffic island
viii] On a cycle track or in a tram lane
ix] Opposite another parked vehicle
x] In a space reserved for local residents? **[See also Rule 239]**

PARKING AT NIGHT AND IN FOG

142] *Which way can you park at night, in the direction of the traffic flow or against it?*

143]144] *Which of these vehicles need to have sidelights on when parked at night?*
i] Vehicles parked in foggy conditions.
ii] Vehicles parked on a road with a 30 mph speed limit
iii] Motorcycles
iv] Invalid carriages
v] Vehicles with projecting loads
vi] Trailers
vii] Goods vehicles or cars of less than 1,525 kgs unladen

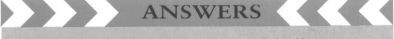

ANSWERS

139A] Either near the kerb or at the entry to a controlled parking zone.
139B]140]141] i]iii] iv] v] vii] viii] No. **viii]** You must not park, either, where you would obstruct trams or force other drivers to enter a tram lane to get round you. **ii]** Yes, but no nearer than 10 meters [32 feet] **vi]** Yes **ix]** Yes, but only where this would not cause an obstruction **x]** Yes, but only if you are a resident in that area with specific permission and a badge to prove it.

PARKING AT NIGHT AND IN FOG
142] With the traffic flow
143]144] i] Yes **ii]** No, unless they are vehicles like **iii] iv]** and **vii]** and are at least 20 meters [32 feet] from a junction and parked by the kerb in the direction of the traffic flow. **iii] iv] vii]** See Answer to **ii] v]** Yes **vi]** Yes

Driving

LOADING AND UNLOADING

145] *Can you load or unload at places where parking is otherwise restricted?*

146] *Can goods vehicles [maximum laden weight over 7.5 tonnes] be parked on a central reservation, verge or footway?*

ROAD WORKS

**** 147]148] *There are road works ahead. If you are driving on a motorway, one or more lanes may be closed. When do you switch lanes to account for this obstruction?*

BREAKDOWNS AND ACCIDENTS

**** 149]150A] *While driving on a motorway, your car has broken down, but you manage to get it onto the hard shoulder. Apart from using your hazard warning lights [See Rule 134] you have placed a red warning triangle 50 meters [164 feet] from your car. What have you done wrong?*

ANSWERS

LOADING AND UNLOADING
145] Yes, but only between times indicated by yellow lines painted across the kerb and set out on nearby sign-plates.
146] Yes, but only if essential for loading and unloading. Otherwise, police permission is required for parking on a central reservation.
ROAD WORKS
147]148] Switch lanes as soon as you can safely do so after seeing the lane indicators which help traffic past the obstruction. Do not drive inside an area marked off by traffic cones, or exceed the temporary speed limit shown on nearby signs.
BREAKDOWNS AND ACCIDENTS
149]150A] Placing the red warning triangle 50 metres [164 feet] in front of your car applies to breakdowns on ordinary roads, not motorways. On the hard shoulder, the triangle should be at least 150 metres [492 feet] away.

Driving

150B] *If you break down at night or when visibility is bad, why should you or your passengers **NOT** stand behind your vehicle while waiting for assistance?*

**** 151] *Something has fallen from your car.*
When should you stop to retrieve it?
i] on an ordinary road
ii] on a motorway
  [See also Rule 170]

**** 152] *Warning signs, lights flashing on emergency vehicles, slow moving or halted traffic in the distance can mean ... **WHAT?***
And what should you do in these circumstances?

ANSWERS

150B] Because your rear lights, which could warn other road users, may not be visible to them.
151] i] Only when it is safe to do so. **ii]** You should not stop at all. If the object could be dangerous, drive to the next emergency telephone and inform the police.
152] There may be an accident up ahead. Slow down and be prepared to stop.

*A*ccidents

**** 153A] *You have been involved in an accident, or have stopped to give assistance. You switch on your warning lights, telephone the emergency services with details of the location and any casualties. You help get the injured and uninjured from their vehicles and wait until the emergency services arrive. One of the injured is a motorcyclist and you remove his helmet to make him more comfortable.*
What have you forgotten to do and what have you done wrong?

153B] *After an accident between your car and another, the other driver requests your name and address if you own the vehicle, or otherwise the owner's name and address. You reply that you will give this information only to the police; in addition, you object when the other driver makes a note of your registration number.*
Have you acted correctly?

153C] *Two days after the accident, where you have NOT given your name and address and registration number, you report the matter to the police.*
Have you acted correctly?

ACCIDENTS INVOLVING DANGEROUS GOODS
**** 154] *In an accident involving vehicles carrying dangerous goods there are special dangers present.*
What are they?

ANSWERS

153A] You have forgotten to ask nearby drivers to switch off their engines and put out cigarettes [in case of fire]. Injured people should not be moved unless fire or explosion is imminent. Most specifically, do not remove an injured motorcyclist's helmet: if he has spinal injuries, you could paralyse him for life.
153B] No. The other driver in an accident has reasonable grounds for requesting the information which the police may also require from you.
153C] In reporting to the police, Yes, but the time limit for this is 24 hours.

ACCIDENTS INVOLVING DANGEROUS GOODS
154] Dangerous substances might escape and uninjured people need to get to a place where the wind will not blow these in their direction. Rescuers can also be affected while assisting the injured at the scene.

First Aid

FIRST AID [FA]

FA1: *Where a person injured in an accident has stopped breathing, you should remove any obvious obstructions from the mouth and tilt the head forwards or backwards?*

FA2: *Apart from a resumption of breathing, what other sign may show the injured person is improving?*

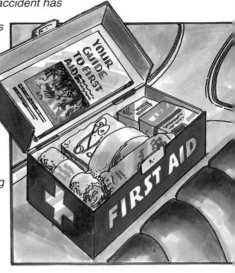

FA3: *How can you stop the bleeding from an injury?*
i] By raising the affected part of the body?
ii] By dabbing the wound with a clean cloth?
iii] By pressing firmly on clean material covering the wound?
iv] By bandaging the wound?

FA4: *What must you check before moving or raising an injured arm or leg?*

FA 5] *To comfort an injured person while awaiting the ambulance should you*
i]Give them a cup of tea
ii] Keep talking to them
iii] Leave them alone, but keep an eye on them
iv] Cover them up to keep them warm?

CARRY A FIRST AID KIT IN YOUR CAR, AND LEARN FIRST AID.

►►► ANSWERS ◄◄◄

FA1: Backwards

FA2: Face colour recovers.

FA3: i] Raise injured limbs as long as they are not broken **ii]** No. **iii]** Yes. **iv]** Yes, after placing a pad over the wound.

FA4: That the arm or leg is not broken.

FA5: i] No. Do not give an injured person anything to drink. **ii]** Yes, to reassure them. **iii]** Never leave an injured person alone. **iv]** Yes.

*M*otorways

MOTORWAYS

155] *Which of the following road users are allowed to use motorways?*
i] Horse riders.
ii] Tractors and other agricultural vehicles.
iii] Pedal cyclists.
iv] Learner drivers.
v] Minicabs or taxis.
vi] Motorcycles under 50 cc. engine capacity.
vii] Provisional ordinary license holders.
viii] Invalid carriages of over 254 kg. unladen weight.
ix] Any slow moving vehicle carrying oversized loads.
x] Pedestrians.

156] *What is the special factor which makes motorway driving different from driving on ordinary roads?*

157] *Complete this checklist as you would when preparing to drive on a motorway:*

Tyres — correct pressure

Oil —...

Water —..

Petrol — enough in the tank?

Mirrors — Clean? Lights - Clean and operating

    properly?

Windows — ....

Reflectors —...

Windscreen — ....

Windscreen washer bottle —........................

158] *What is a slip road?*
159] *If a slip road continues as an extra lane alongside the motorway, when do you move onto the motorway itself?*
160] Should you overtake other cars as soon as you get onto the motorway?

ANSWERS

MOTORWAYS

155] v] viii] [but only with police permission] **iii]** and **vii]** [but only in an emergency]

156] The special factor is speed. Traffic moves much more quickly on motorways than it does on ordinary roads.

157] Oil / Water: check there is enough. Windows / Reflectors / Windscreen clean? Windscreen washer bottle: Topped up?

158] A road that leads, from the left, onto a motorway.

159] When the slip road merges with the motorway.

160] No. Wait until you have become accustomed to the speed of the traffic before overtaking.

*M*otorways  RULES 161-165

ON THE MOTORWAY

GOOD FOOD
Puddleworth
Services ½ m

Petrol 46.5 p

161] *At what speed should you drive when on the motorway?*
i] The same speed as other drivers.
ii] More slowly than other drivers.
iii] At up to 70 mph.
iv] At a steady cruising speed you feel comfortable with as long as it is neither too fast nor too slow.
v] At up to 60 mph.
[See also Question for Rules 57/58]

162] *If you want to stop because you feel sleepy - very easy, given the monotony of much motorway driving - should you pull over to the hard shoulder for a rest?*

163] *You have missed your exit on the motorway. Do you*
i] Reverse and drive back to it the way you have come?
ii] Cross the central reservation and drive back to your exit on the opposite motorway lane?
iii] Carry on to the next exit and work your way back by the ordinary road system?
iv] Carry on to the next exit, re-enter the motorway system and drive back to the exit you wanted in the first place?

LANE DISCIPLINE

164] *In ordinary circumstances, which lane may you use to overtake on the motorway?*
[See also Question for Rule 167]

165] *How can you avoid being "carried off" the motorway before you have reached your chosen exit?*

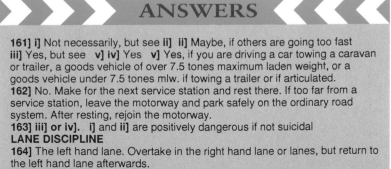

ANSWERS

161] i] Not necessarily, but see **ii] ii]** Maybe, if others are going too fast **iii]** Yes, but see **v] iv]** Yes **v]** Yes, if you are driving a car towing a caravan or trailer, a goods vehicle of over 7.5 tones maximum laden weight, or a goods vehicle under 7.5 tones mlw. if towing a trailer or if articulated.
162] No. Make for the next service station and rest there. If too far from a service station, leave the motorway and park safely on the ordinary road system. After resting, rejoin the motorway.
163] iii] or iv]. **i]** and **ii]** are positively dangerous if not suicidal
LANE DISCIPLINE
164] The left hand lane. Overtake in the right hand lane or lanes, but return to the left hand lane afterwards.
165] By making sure you are in the proper lane for driving on. Watch motorway signs and markings.

Motorways

RULES 166-173

166] *Which of these vehicles must NOT use the right hand lane of a three-lane or more than three-lane motorway?*
i] Taxis
ii] Vans
iii] A car drawing a trailer
iv] A goods vehicle with a maximum laden weight of 6.5 tonnes
v] Buses
vi] A lorry drawing a trailer
vii] Coaches
viii] A goods vehicle with maximum laden weight of 8.5 tonnes

OVERTAKING

167] i] *Can you overtake on the motorway if you are already in the left-hand lane and are moving faster than the traffic on your right?*
ii] *Can you use the hard shoulder to overtake?*

168] SEE QUESTION AND ANSWER TO RULES NO. 99 169]
SEE QUESTION AND ANSWER TO RULES NO. 164

MOTORWAY SIGNALS

170] *Where will you normally find motorway signals warning of an accident, a slippery surface or other danger ahead?*

171] *A flashing amber signal on the motorway means danger ahead and there may be a speed limit or a message such as FOG. You slow down accordingly. When is it safe to speed up again?*

172]173] *On the motorway, what do you do if you see a red light flashing*
i] above your lane
ii] on the central reservation or slip road?

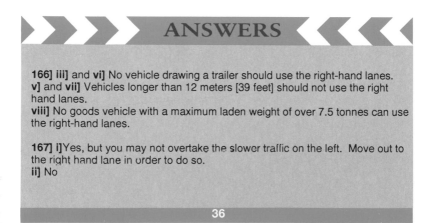

ANSWERS

166] iii] and **vi]** No vehicle drawing a trailer should use the right-hand lanes.
v] and **vii]** Vehicles longer than 12 meters [39 feet] should not use the right hand lanes.
viii] No goods vehicle with a maximum laden weight of over 7.5 tonnes can use the right-hand lanes.

167] i] Yes, but you may not overtake the slower traffic on the left. Move out to the right hand lane in order to do so.
ii] No

*M*otorways

ROAD STUDS AND SIGNS

174] TRUE or FALSE] *Two of these statements are wrong*:
i] Amber-coloured studs mark the left-hand edge of the motorway.
ii] Green studs mark the edge of the slip road.
iii] Red studs mark the left-hand edge.
iv] White studs mark the separate lanes on the motorway.

ANSWERS

MOTORWAY SIGNALS
170] On the central reservation or overhead.
171] After you have passed the danger spot **AND** see a signal which is not flashing.
172]173] i] You change lanes to one without a flashing red signal. This signal means you must not drive beyond it.
ii] Red lights flashing at the central reservation or slip road mean you cannot drive on in any of the motorway lanes.

ROAD STUDS AND SIGNS
174] i] is **FALSE:** amber-coloured studs mark the right-hand edge.
v] is **FALSE:** Green studs mark the edge of the slip road.

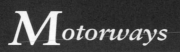

Motorways

175] *If you want to change lanes on a motorway, when should you prepare to do so?*

176] SEE QUESTIONS FOR RULE 58

ROAD WORKS

177] SEE QUESTIONS FOR RULE 147

OBSTRUCTIONS

178] SEE QUESTIONS FOR RULE 151

STOPPING AND PARKING

179] *What are the exceptions to the rule that you must not stop on a motorway?*

180] *While on the motorway, where can you park?*

181] *A hitch hiker standing by the slip road signals that s/he wants a lift. You want to oblige.* **Should you?**

182] SEE QUESTIONS FOR RULE 155

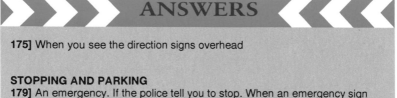

175] When you see the direction signs overhead

STOPPING AND PARKING
179] An emergency. If the police tell you to stop. When an emergency sign shows. When flashing red light signals show

180] Nowhere. The carriageway, slip road and hard shoulder **[except in an emergency]** are not for parking. You can park only in the service stations off the motorway.

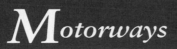

*M*otorways

RULE 183

BREAKDOWNS

183A] *Here is a set of rules for what to do when you break down on the motorway, but cannot reach a service area.*
What has been left out?
What is wrong?

Try to stop near one of the emergency telephones sited about a mile apart along the hard shoulder. You pull in as far to the left as possible on the hard shoulder, then you and your passengers, together with your dog, get out by the left-hand doors. They wait, standing at the rear of the car, while you walk to the nearest emergency telephone and call the police. If you are a woman travelling alone or with child passengers, say so.

ANSWERS

181] No. The slip road is part of the motorway and you must not pick up or set down passengers anywhere on a motorway.

BREAKDOWNS
183A] You have forgotten to switch on your hazard warning lights [and sidelights at night or in bad visibility] You should not let dogs or any other animal out of your car. They should remain inside. The rear of your car is too close to the motorway for passengers to stand. They should wait well back from it.

Motorways / Cyclists

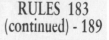

RULES 183
(continued) - 189

183B] *Suppose you cannot get your broken down vehicle onto the hard shoulder.* **Do you:**

i] Switch on hazard warning lights

ii] Place a red warning triangle on the carriageway to warn other drivers

iii] Attempt to repair the car

iv] Wait in the car for the emergency services to arrive?

183C] *Disabled drivers who cannot leave their cars should switch on hazard warning lights, stay in the car with the doors locked - and what else?*

184] *The car is repaired. You are ready to resume your journey. You drive on along the hard shoulder, building up speed, and having checked the lane, signal and turn right to rejoin the motorway. Have you done the right things?*

LEAVING THE MOTORWAY

185] *How do you know from signs on the motorway that you are approaching your chosen exit?*

186] *Once on the slip road, what is the first thing you should do?*

EXTRA RULES FOR CYCLISTS

187] **BICYCLE CARE:** *Match up the items in the two columns [there may be more than one answer]*

BICYCLE FEATURE:	**SHOULD BE KEPT:**
i] chain	**a]** in good working order
ii] tyres	**b]** in correct working condition
iii] brakes and gears	**c]** well oiled
iv] lights and reflectors	**d]** in good condition
v] saddle	**e]** at proper adjustment or height
	f] clean

189] *Why is a bicycle bell important?*

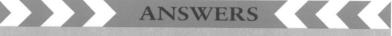

ANSWERS

183B] i] Yes. **ii]** No [you should not get out of the car unless you can get off the carriageway safely] **iii]** No **iv]** Yes - wearing your seat belt.

183C] Display a **HELP** pennant and, if available, use a mobile telephone to call the emergency services.

184] Yes. You should always build up speed before rejoining the motorway so as to match the speed of other traffic.

LEAVING THE MOTORWAY185] By directional signs naming the places served by the exit and by roadside "countdown" markers - three white strips for 300 yards to the exit, two for 200 yards and one for 100 yards, all on blue background.

186] Check your speed. Motorway driving can be deceptive, making 50 mph seem like only 30 mph. Remember that speeds on the ordinary roads ahead are much slower.

EXTRA RULES FOR CYCLISTS 187] i] c] and e] **ii]** a] ensure, too, that tyres are properly inflated: follow the manufacturer's recommendation **iii]** b] **iv]** a and f] **v]** e]

189] Like a car horn, a bell warns other road users and alerts blind or partially sighted pedestrians to your presence.

Cyclists / Horseriders RULES 190-197

SAFETY EQUIPMENT AND CLOTHING

190] 191] *You must carry front and rear lights and a red rear reflector on your bicycle, but which of the following are* **NOT** *recommended for cyclists?*

i] "Spacer" flags
ii] Long coats
iii Long scarves
iv] Dark visors
v] Fluorescent clothing
vi] Light-coloured clothing
vii] Any cycle helmet
viii] Reflective belts and arm-or ankle-bands
ix] Wheel reflectors

CYCLING

192] *Suppose you are approaching red traffic lights and like other road traffic, you are required to stop. Can you cycle on the pavement to get round the lights?*

193] *You are about to move away from the kerb or, while moving along, intend to turn or maneuver. What must you do before you embark on any of these if you are a cyclist or horserider*

194]195] *You need to watch well ahead to avoid drains, parked cars, pot holes or features designed to slow traffic down such as road humps or narrowing. However, what extra danger do parked cars pose to cyclists?*

196] *Why should you not leave your bicycle lying on the pavement or in the road? Because:*

i] It could be damaged
ii] The police will remove it
iii] It obstructs and endangers other road users or pedestrians.

197] *A long vehicle is in front of you, signalling a left turn into a side road. You want to go straight on.* **Do you overtake on the left or on the right?**

ANSWERS

SAFETY EQUIPMENT AND CLOTHING 190]191] NOT recommended: **ii]** and **iii]** can get caught up in the chain or wheel **iv]** would reduce your vision **vii]** You should not wear just **ANY** helmet, but one which conforms to accepted safety standards.

CYCLING192] No. Cycling on the pavement is a danger to pedestrians and is not permitted. However, at some road junctions, cyclists can get ahead of other traffic by using advance stop lines

193] Look all round to ensure the road is clear and there is a suitable gap in the traffic. When you are sure it is safe, give other road users a clear arm signal to let them know what you are going to do.

194] 195] The nearside doors may be opened in your path. Leave plenty of room on your left just in case when cycling past parked cars.

196] i] and **ii]** are possible, but **iii]** is the important answer.

197] Neither. Wait until the long vehicle has completed its turn in front of you before riding on. The same applies on roundabouts: it is safer to wait until a long vehicle has cleared the roundabout.

*C*yclists / *H*orseriders

RULES 198-207

198] *Car drivers can move to a safe place in the centre of the road while waiting to turn right. Should cyclists do the same?*

SIGNAL CONTROL JUNCTIONS

199] SEE QUESTIONS FOR RULE NO 192

ROUNDABOUTS

200] *If you are a cyclist or horserider, you may feel safer going round in the left hand lane of a roundabout, that is round the outside edge. This, however, brings you directly across exits off the roundabout which other traffic may wish to use. How do you let other traffic know which exit you are going to take?*

201] SEE ANSWER TO QUESTION FOR RULE NO.197

202] SEE ANSWER TO QUESTION FOR RULE NO.198

BUS LANES
203] *When can a cyclist use a bus lane?*

DUAL CARRIAGEWAYS
204] *You are riding on a fast road where there are no traffic signals, but you want to cross the road or make a right turn. How should you proceed on*
i] a dual carriageway
ii] a motorway?

CYCLE LANES AND TRACKS

205] 206] *Cycle lanes, which you should use wherever possible, are marked along carriageways by*
i] a broken line
ii] an unbroken line

207] SEE ANSWER TO QUESTIONS FOR RULE NO. 205 — 206

>>> **ANSWERS** <<<

198] No. It is better to wait on the left until a safe gap appears, or you can walk your bicycle across the road instead. On roundabouts, it may be safer to dismount and walk your machine round the verge or pavement, if there is one

ROUNDABOUTS 200] By signalling right while passing across each exit you do not want to take. Then signal left before the desired exit.

BUS LANES 203] When it displays a cycle symbol.
DUAL CARRIAGEWAYS 204] i] Be watchful and cross each carriageway as if it were a separate road. **ii]** Pedal cyclists are not permitted on motorways.

CYCLE LANES AND TRACKS
205]206] Either, but **SEE QUESTIONS FOR RULE 98** for possible behaviour of other traffic.

Cyclists / Animals

208] *There may be two cycle tracks, one on each side of the road. If you want to cross from one to the other, do you use [if available]:*
i] a crossing with traffic lights
ii] a pedestrian Pelican crossing
iii] a crossing with light signals showing a green cycle symbol?

SAFE RIDING
209]210]211] *Three cyclists are riding along a road next to each other. One has a passenger who sits on a parcel rack behind the rider. Another is drinking a can of low-alcohol beer as he rides along. The cyclists are preparing to overtake a vehicle a foot or two in front of them on the left-hand lane. All three have both feet on the pedals. The cyclist nearest the middle of the road signals the overtaking maneuver with his right hand.*
WHAT IS WRONG WITH THIS SCENARIO?

ANIMALS
212] 213] *You have a calm-natured dog who is accustomed to being walked or driven in traffic.*
Should you:
i] keep the dog on a short lead while walking along a road?
ii] let it walk without a lead or on its own?
iii] keep it on a long lead while walking?
iv] pat the dog while driving?
v] put a lead on the dog before getting out of the car?

214] *If two or more people are herding animals, and are close to the brow of a hill, one should go ahead. Why?*

215] SEE QUESTIONS FOR RULE NO. [5A]

►►► ANSWERS ◄◄◄

208] iii]
SAFE RIDING 209]210]211] The cyclists should be riding no more than two abreast **[see RULE 209]** and if on a cycle track or narrow road, should keep to single file only. The cycle with the passenger is not built or adapted to carry one.**[RULE 210]** No one should ride a bicycle when under the influence of drink or drugs **[RULE 211]** The beer-drinker is also breaking the rule that both hands should be kept on the handlebars, except when signalling or changing gear **[RULE 209]**. In addition, all three are cycling far too close to the vehicle in front **[RULE 209]**

ANIMALS 212] 213] i] Yes. This also applies to walking on a footpath next to a cycle track **[RULE 212]**. **ii]** No. **iii]** No. **iv]** No: you should not let the dog distract you while driving **v]** Yes
214] To warn other road users who may not be able to see the herd approaching.

*H*orse riders / *R*ailways   RULES 216-225

HORSE RIDERS
216 - 219] and **224]** *Check list for horseriders. What has been omitted?*

BEFORE SETTING OUT:
Make sure the saddle and other tack fits well [Bareback riding is not allowed on the road] Wear reflective clothing at night. Wear boots or shoes with hard soles and heels. Wear an approved safety helmet.

WHILE RIDING
Keep both hands on the reins unless signalling. Do not wear long clothing or anything else that might get tangled up in the reins. Wear light-coloured or fluorescent clothing.

220] *When leading a horse, do you keep it on your left or your right?*

221] 222] *When on the road, may horseriders :*
i] move in single file
ii] ride three abreast
iii] use the pavement
iv] use foot paths
v] ride two abreast
vi] use a bridle-path
vii] use a cycle track ?

223] SEE QUESTIONS FOR RULE NO. 200]

RAILWAY LEVEL CROSSINGS

225A] *The barriers at a railway level crossing are down, but there is no sign of a train. You wait. Still no train. Should you:*
i] zigzag round the barriers and across the rail line?
ii] go on waiting
iii] drive up closer to the track to see if the train is coming ?

≫≫≫ ANSWERS ≪≪≪

HORSERIDERS
216-219] and **224]** Your horse should also wear reflective clothing i.e. reflective bands on its legs above the fetlock joints. Make sure your helmet is securely fastened: this is obligatory for children under fourteen. Keep both feet in the stirrups. Do not carry a passenger. Fluorescent clothing is suitable for the daytime: wear reflective clothing at night.
220] On the left
221]222] i] necessary on narrow roads. **ii]** too many **iii]** No **iv]** No **v]** two abreast is permitted on most ordinary roads **vi]** Yes, if available **vii]** No.

RAILWAY LEVEL CROSSINGS
225A] i] and **iii]** Definitely not **[Rule 228] ii]** Yes

*R*ailways

225B] *The barriers are up and the road ahead is clear, but the car in front of you seems to be taking an age to drive over the level crossing.*
Should you follow?
226] *Which of the following features will you find at level crossings? Two other features have been omitted.* **What are they?**
i] full barriers
ii] one steady red light
iii] a flashing amber light
iv] half barriers
v] green **GO** lights
vi] one red flashing light
vii] two red flashing lights
viii] a steady amber light
ix] gates or barriers, but no lights
x] red and green lights together and **STOP** signs.?
227] *A train goes by, but the red lights are still flashing, the barriers remain down and the audible alarm is making a different sound.*
What is happening here?
228] SEE QUESTIONS FOR RULE NO. 225]

RAILWAY TELEPHONES
229] *A sign at a level crossing instructs you to obtain permission to cross by using a special telephone. You are told to telephone again once you have crossed. What are you driving if you have to observe this rule?*

►►► ANSWERS ◄◄◄

225B] No. Never drive nose to tail across a level crossing. Wait until the car in front has cleared the track and there is room for you to drive straight across without stopping.
226] i]iv] ix] Most level crossings have either full or half barriers. Some have gates or barriers, but no lights: here you must stop when the barriers come down, or close. **iii] vii] viii]** Yes.   **v] x]** At some unattended crossings where you open and close the gates or barriers yourself, a red light indicates train approaching. The green light indicates the track is clear and you may cross. Afterwards, do remember to close the gates on both sides **[Rule 232]** Features omitted: The audible alarm and the white line on the road where you must stop when the amber light shows or the alarm sounds. If already across the white line, keep going.
227] Another train is coming.
RAILWAY TELEPHONES
229] A slow moving vehicle or a herd of animals

Railways / Tramways   RULES 230-241

ACCIDENTS OR BREAKDOWNS

230] Your vehicle has broken down on a level crossing. There is no railway telephone to enable you to get in touch with the signal operator and obtain instructions, but everyone has got clear of the vehicle. Suddenly, the alarm sounds and the amber light comes on. A train is coming.
Should you

i] try to push your vehicle off the track?
ii] attempt to restart the engine and drive it off the track?
iii] get off the railway line?

CROSSING WITHOUT LIGHTS
231]232] SEE QUESTION FOR RULE NO. 226

UNATTENDED CROSSINGS WITHOUT SIGNALS/OPEN CROSSINGS

233] 234] There are two other types of level crossing not already covered. Here, you have to look both ways and listen to make sure no train is coming before you can cross. Neither of these crossings has light signals or attendants but one does have a **GIVE WAY** sign.
Describe these level crossings.

TRAMWAYS

235]236] 237]238A]239]240] 241A] There are six possible clues which tell you that a road has trams running along it. **What are they?**

238B] A tram has halted at a stop with no platform.
You want to overtake. Can you do so:

i] on the left
ii] on the right
iii] on either side ??

239] SEE QUESTIONS FOR RULES NOS. 139 - 141.

ANSWERS

ACCIDENTS AND BREAKDOWNS 230] i] No   ii] No   iii] Yes
UNATTENDED CROSSINGS WITHOUT SIGNALS/OPEN CROSSINGS
233] 234] The crossing with the **GIVE WAY** sign is an open crossing with no gates or barriers. The other level crossing has gates which you open and close yourself. Here, you may be able to use a railway telephone to contact a signal operator who can tell you when it is safe to cross. Use the telephone again to let the operator know when you have done so.

TRAMWAYS 235]236] 237]238A]239]240] 241A] *Clue 1:* Special tram lanes in the roadway, sometimes marked by white lines *Clue 2:* A surface for trams different from the rest of the road, with shallow kerbs in pedestrian areas **[RULE 241]** *Clue 3:* Two sorts of traffic lights, one for tram drivers, the other for the rest of the road users. *Clue 4:* Diamond shaped signs giving instructions to tram drivers only [this road is for trams only] *Clue 5:* A special platform for tram stops, at the centre or the side of the road *Clue 6:* Rail tracks running from one side of the road to the other, or close to the kerb where the road narrows.
238B] The correct answer is ii]. However it is particularly dangerous to drive between a tram and the left hand kerb[i]

Tramways

PEDESTRIANS

241B] 242] *Some tram tracks are unfenced and pedestrians may cross at any point.
Elsewhere, at special crossing places, what colour lights flash to warn pedestrians that a tram is coming and they should not cross until it has passed by?*
[See also Answer toQuestion for Rule No.14 [b]]

>>> **ANSWERS** <<<

PEDESTRIANS

241B] 242] Flashing amber lights.

Traffic Signals

TRAFFIC LIGHT SIGNALS
THE FIRST THREE QUESTIONS REFER TO THE FIVE SETS OF TRAFFIC LIGHTS AT THE TOP OF THE OPPOSITE PAGE.

1] Which of the traffic light signals mean STOP?
2] What does the green arrow indicate on the fifth set of traffic lights shown?
3] Which other signal shown here will be displayed when traffic turning left AND going straight ahead may both proceed?

FLASHING RED LIGHTS

4] *THIS SIGNAL [6 opposite page] is seen at railway level crossings ... and where else?* **Give three locations.**

MOTORWAY SIGNALS

5] *The captions to the motorway signals, illustrated opposite [A - H] have been muddled up.* **Sort them out.**

A] LANE AHEAD CLOSED [i]
B] REDUCED VISIBILITY AHEAD [ii]
C] END OF RESTRICTION [iii]
D] DO NOT PROCEED FURTHER IN THIS LANE [iv]
E] TEMPORARY MAXIMUM SPEED LIMIT [v]
F] LEAVE MOTORWAY AT NEXT EXIT [vi]
G] TEMPORARY MAXIMUM SPEED LIMIT/INFO. [vii]
H] CHANGE LANE [viii]

LANE CONTROL SIGNALS

6] *The "bridge" of signals shown opposite is a set of overhead motorway lane controls. Here, a red cross means LANE CLOSED TO TRAFFIC. What does the green arrow pointing downward indicate? What does a white diagonal arrow signify?*

ANSWERS

TRAFFIC LIGHT SIGNALS

1:1] red only signal **2]** red and amber, but green for **GO** is about to show and **4]** amber only, but red for **STOP** is about to show.
2: Figure 5 Traffic turning can go, but traffic intending to drive straight on must wait
3: Signal No. 3

FLASHING RED LIGHTS

4: Lifting bridges, fire stations and airfields.

Traffic Signals

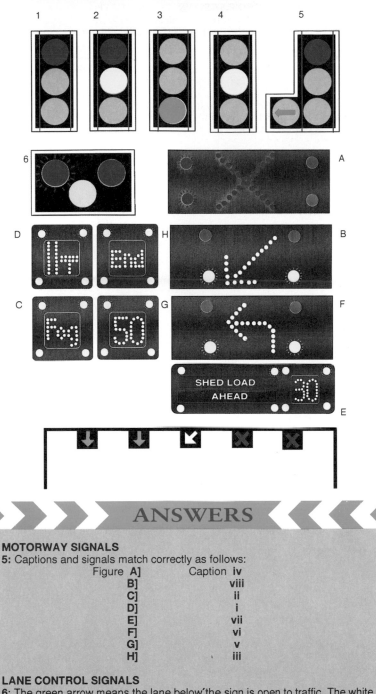

MOTORWAY SIGNALS

5: Captions and signals match correctly as follows:

Figure	Caption
A]	iv
B]	viii
C]	ii
D]	i
E]	vii
F]	vi
G]	v
H]	iii

LANE CONTROL SIGNALS

6: The green arrow means the lane below the sign is open to traffic. The white diagonal arrow means you should change the direction indicated.

Traffic Signals

SIGNALS BY AUTHORISED PERSONS

1: *What is the connection between* **Figure 3** *and the other two pictures?*

BECKONING TRAFFIC ON

2: *Which of these signals Figs. 4 & 5 indicates*

i] Beckoning traffic on from the side and which indicates
ii] Beckoning traffic on from the front.
iii] What does **Figure 6** signify?

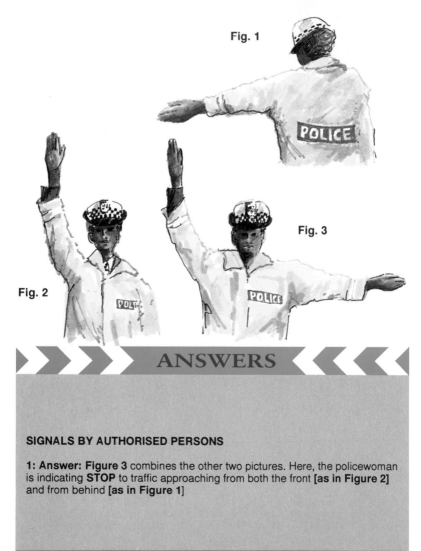

Fig. 1

Fig. 2

Fig. 3

ANSWERS

SIGNALS BY AUTHORISED PERSONS

1: Answer: Figure 3 combines the other two pictures. Here, the policewoman is indicating **STOP** to traffic approaching from both the front **[as in Figure 2]** and from behind **[as in Figure 1]**

50

*T*raffic *S*ignals

Fig. 5

Fig. 4

Fig. 6

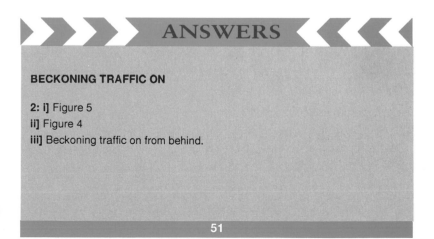

ANSWERS

BECKONING TRAFFIC ON

2: i] Figure 5
ii] Figure 4
iii] Beckoning traffic on from behind.

Traffic Signals

DIRECTION INDICATOR SIGNALS

1: Figure 1
This direction indicator signal means: "I intend to move out to the right or...?

2: Figure 2
This signal means 'I intend to turn left or stop on the left and...?

BRAKE LIGHT SIGNALS

3: Figure 3
When this signal appears on the vehicle in front, what has the driver or rider done to activate it - and why?

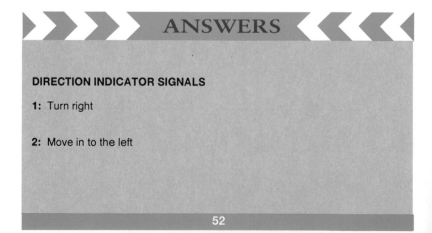

ANSWERS

DIRECTION INDICATOR SIGNALS

1: Turn right

2: Move in to the left

*T*raffic *S*ignals

Figure 1

Figure 2

Figure 3

>>> **ANSWERS** <<<

BRAKE LIGHT SIGNALS

3: The brake has been touched or applied. In both cases, the signal means **"I am slowing down or stopping."**

Traffic Signals

1: Which of these arm signals [Figs. 1 and 3] means the driver is about to move in to the left or turn left?

2: A motorcycle rider indicates a right turn in the same way as a car driver. Do both use:
i] the same **TURN LEFT** signal?
ii] The same signal for "I intend to stop or slow down"?

ARM SIGNALS TO PERSONS CONTROLLING TRAFFIC

3: When signalling to persons controlling traffic, car drivers give arm signals to the right **[Figure 9]** or the left **[Figure 8]** to show in which direction they mean to turn.
i] How do drivers signal that they mean to drive straight on?
ii] What will tell a traffic controller of an impending right or left turn?

Figure 7   Figure 8   Figure 9

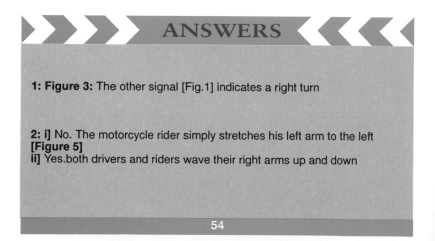

>>>>> **ANSWERS** <<<<<

1: Figure 3: The other signal [Fig.1] indicates a right turn

2: i] No. The motorcycle rider simply stretches his left arm to the left **[Figure 5]**
ii] Yes.both drivers and riders wave their right arms up and down

*T*raffic *S*ignals

Figure 1

Figure 2

Figure 3

Figure 4

Figure 5

Figure 6

ANSWERS

ARM SIGNALS TO PERSONS CONTROLLING TRAFFIC

3: i] left arm, bent at the elbow, pointing straight up **[Figure 7]**
ii] Direction indicator lights

Traffic Signals

1: *These signs giving orders are grouped by type.* **What sort of order does each group signify?**

i] Figures 1,2,3 and 5

ii] Figures 6, 7, 14, 17

2: *How does Figure 17 differ from the other signals in the same group, even though its significance is the same?*

3: *What do these signs have in common?*
Figures 8, 9, 15, 16, 18, 19, 20, 21, 22, 23, 24

4: *Figure 27: Does this sign indicate*
i] No stopping
ii] Stop
iii] Lane closed ahead?

5: *Which of these signals indicates* **NO U — TURN ?**
Figures 10, 11, 12

6: *Figure 13: What can you* **NOT** *do when you see this sign?*

7: *Figures 23, 24, 25, 26: What do these signs limit in vehicles using the roads on which they appear?*

8: *Figure 28 What kind of sign is this?*

9: *Figure 29. This is a No Stopping sign, but why are times shown on it?*

10: *Figure 30. What is ended by this sign?*

11: *Figs. 31, 32, 33. What sort of traffic is prohibited by these signs?*

ANSWERS

1: i] Speed limitation. **Figure 5** indicates that the national speed limit applies
ii] They all give orders to halt or give way. **Figure 14** means that traffic from the opposite direction has priority.

2: Figure 17 is a temporary sign manually operated at, for instance, road works. The other signs are fixed.

3: They prohibit entry by certain road users viz: **Figure 8**: No vehicles
Figure 9: No entry for vehicular traffic. **Figure 15**: No motor vehicles.
Figure 16: No motor vehicles except solo motorcycles, scooters or mopeds. **Figure 18:** No vehicles over twelve seats except regular scheduled school and work buses. **Figure 19:** No cycling **Figure 20:** No pedestrians.
Figure 21: No goods vehicles over maximum gross weight shown.
Figure 22: No goods vehicles or combination of vehicles over the length shown. **Figure 23:** No vehicles over the height shown. **Figure 24:** No vehicles over the width shown.

4: ii]

Traffic Signals

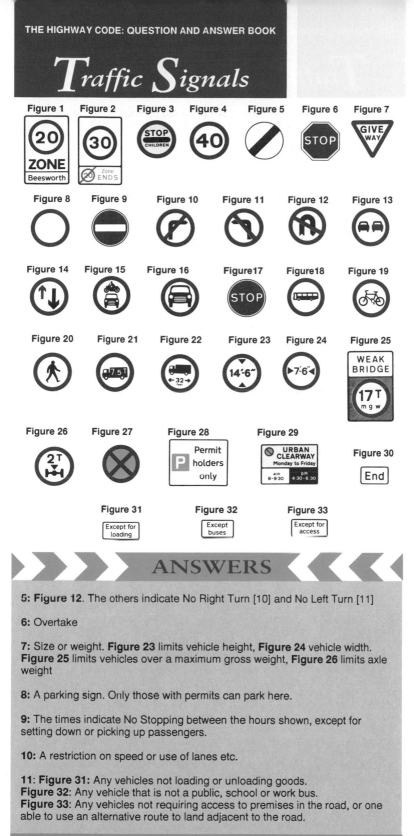

Figure 1, Figure 2, Figure 3, Figure 4, Figure 5, Figure 6, Figure 7, Figure 8, Figure 9, Figure 10, Figure 11, Figure 12, Figure 13, Figure 14, Figure 15, Figure 16, Figure 17, Figure 18, Figure 19, Figure 20, Figure 21, Figure 22, Figure 23, Figure 24, Figure 25, Figure 26, Figure 27, Figure 28, Figure 29, Figure 30, Figure 31, Figure 32, Figure 33

ANSWERS

5: Figure 12. The others indicate No Right Turn [10] and No Left Turn [11]

6: Overtake

7: Size or weight. **Figure 23** limits vehicle height, **Figure 24** vehicle width. **Figure 25** limits vehicles over a maximum gross weight, **Figure 26** limits axle weight

8: A parking sign. Only those with permits can park here.

9: The times indicate No Stopping between the hours shown, except for setting down or picking up passengers.

10: A restriction on speed or use of lanes etc.

11: Figure 31: Any vehicles not loading or unloading goods.
Figure 32: Any vehicle that is not a public, school or work bus.
Figure 33: Any vehicles not requiring access to premises in the road, or one able to use an alternative route to land adjacent to the road.

Traffic Signals

1: *What is the purpose of most signs with a blue background?*

2: ***Figures 1,2,3,4,5,10,11:*** *Which sign is the odd one out in this group?*

3: ***Figures 6, 12, 13:*** *What do these signs have in common?*

4: ***Figures 7 and 15:*** *What do these signs have in common?*

5: ***Figure 16, 17:*** *What is the difference between these two signs?*

6: ***Figures 8 and 9:*** *How are these signs connected?*

7: ***Figure 14:*** *What happens where you see this sign?*

WARNING SIGNS

8: *Both triangular [with point upwards] and circular signs can have red borders, but what is the basic difference between them?*

9: *As you drive along a [purely imaginary] road, you see these signs in succession. Describe the road. What happens at the end of it?*
Figures 19, 25, 28, 26, 31, 37, 38, 22, 39, 21

10: ***Figures 30,. 31, 32:*** *Which is these is the odd one out?*

11: ***Figure 36:*** *What has happened here?*

12: ***Figures 18,23,29,35:*** *What is the purpose of these signs?*

13: **Figure 24:** This sign tells you that the road is about to bend to the left [or the right if the chevrons are reversed]. Having regard to the uncommon shape of this sign, what else does it tell you?

14: **Figures 33, 34:** These are signs warning of two-way traffic ahead. Where are you likely to find them?

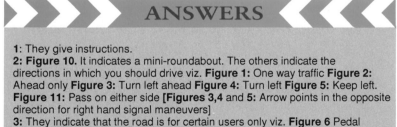

ANSWERS

1: They give instructions.
2: **Figure 10.** It indicates a mini-roundabout. The others indicate the directions in which you should drive viz. **Figure 1:** One way traffic **Figure 2:** Ahead only **Figure 3:** Turn left ahead **Figure 4:** Turn left **Figure 5:** Keep left. **Figure 11:** Pass on either side **[Figures 3,4** and **5:** Arrow points in the opposite direction for right hand signal maneuvers]
3: They indicate that the road is for certain users only viz. **Figure 6** Pedal cyclists **Figure 12:** Buses and cyclists only **Figure 13:** Trams only
4: They signify that only two sorts of road users may use the road i.e. **Figure 7:** Cyclists and pedestrians **Figure 15:** With-flow buses and cycles.
5: **Figure 16** indicates a bus lane moving against the flow of traffic. **Figure 17** indicates a cycle lane moving with the flow of traffic.
6: **Figure 8** means minimum speed. **Figure 9:** means end of minimum speed.
7: There is a pedestrian crossing point over a tramway

Traffic Signals

Figure 1 Figure 2 Figure 3 Figure 4 Figure 5 Figure 6 Figure 7 Figure 8

Figure 9 Figure 10 Figure 11 Figure 12 Figure 13 Figure 14 Figure 15

Figure 16 Figure 17 Figure 18 Figure 19 Figure 20

Figure 21 Figure 22 Figure 23 Figure 24 Figure 25 Figure 26

Figure 27 Figure 28 Figure 29 Figure 30 Figure 31 Figure 32

Figure 33 Figure 34 Figure 35 Figure 36 Figure 37 Figure 38 Figure 39

►►► ANSWERS ◄◄◄

WARNING SIGNS

8: The triangular signs are usually warning signs, the circular signs are usually prohibitive. [An exception is the red-bordered **GIVE WAY** inverted triangle waffic on a major road ahead **[See Figure 7 page 57]**

9] You come to a crossroads **[19]** then the road bends **[25]** The road ahead is uneven **[28]** and next bends to the right **[26]**. Then it narrows **[31]** Watch out for a slippery road surface **[37]** and prepare for a steep downward hill **[38]**. After this, you encounter a staggered junction **[22]**, a steep upward slope **[39]** and finally reach a T- junction **[21]** where you turn right or left depending on your destination.

10: Figure 30: It indicates a dual carriageway. The other two tell you the road is going to narrow, either on the right **[31]** or otherwise both sides **[32]**

11: Traffic signals have failed, so take care.

12: They tell you of actions you must take viz. **18]** Stop at a line 100 yards ahead **23]** Give way 50 yards ahead **29]** Reduce speed now **35]** Read and obey traffic lights.

13: The sign also "says" that the bend is a sharp deviation in the road requiring special care, and usually a reduction in speed as well.

14: On a one-way road: **Figure 33:** Indicates that two way traffic is going to cross a one way road ahead. **Figure 34:** Indicates that traffic becomes two-way straight ahead.

Traffic Signals

1: **Figures 17,18,19 and 20:** All these signs denote the presence of animals in the vicinity, but what is the important difference between **Figures 17 and 20 and Figures 18 and 19?**

2: **Figures 1, 2, 3, 4, 7, and 16:** Who will you find ahead or crossing the road when you see five of these six signs? The sixth is the odd one out. Which is it?

3: **Figures 9,21, and 22:** What do these signs have in common?

4: What is in the vicinity when you see these signs? **Figures 12, 13, 14 and 15.**

5: **Figures 12, 23.** What is in the vicinity when you see these signs?

6: Which are the odd two out among these warning signs? **Figures 8,10,11, 24, 26 ,27, 28 and 29.**

7: What can you expect ahead when you see **Figures 6, 25, 30?.**

8: **Figure 5:** What lies ahead when you see this sign?

►►►►► ANSWERS ◄◄◄◄◄

1: Figures 17 and **20:** denote domesticated animals under control. **Figures 18** and **19** denote wild animals, possibly roaming free.

2 Figure 16: is the odd one out. It denotes trams crossing ahead. The others denote different types of pedestrians ahead i.e. **Figure 1:** Children going to or from school. **Figure 2:** Elderly people, [or blind or disabled as shown] crossing the road. **Figure 3**: Pedestrians in the road ahead. **Figure 4:** Pedestrians crossing. **Figure 7:** Labourers at road works.

3: They warn of dangers involving water. i.e. **Figure 9:** Ford across the road **Figure 21:** A quayside or river bank **Figure 22:** Opening or swing bridge ahead.

4: A level crossing. **Figure 12** Light signals ahead at a level crossing [or bridge or airfield] **Figure 13**: A level crossing with a barrier or gate ahead. **Figure 14:** A level crossing ahead without barrier or gate. **Figure 15**: A level crossing without a barrier.

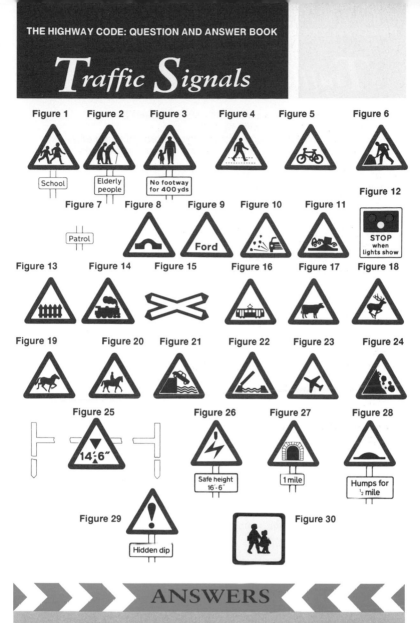

THE HIGHWAY CODE: QUESTION AND ANSWER BOOK

*T*raffic *S*ignals

Figure 1 · **Figure 2** · **Figure 3** · **Figure 4** · **Figure 5** · **Figure 6**

School · Elderly people · No footway for 400 yds

Figure 12

Figure 7 · **Figure 8** · **Figure 9** · **Figure 10** · **Figure 11**

Patrol · Ford · STOP when lights show

Figure 13 · **Figure 14** · **Figure 15** · **Figure 16** · **Figure 17** · **Figure 18**

Figure 19 · **Figure 20** · **Figure 21** · **Figure 22** · **Figure 23** · **Figure 24**

Figure 25 · **Figure 26** · **Figure 27** · **Figure 28**

14'6" · Safe height 16'-6" · 1 mile · Humps for ½ mile

Figure 29

! · Hidden dip

Figure 30

> > > > ANSWERS < < < <

5: An airfield.

6: Figures 24 [falling or fallen rocks] and **Figure 26:** [overhead electric cable] are the odd two out. The other signs denote dangers on or along the road **Figures 24** and **26:** warn of dangers from above. **Figure 8:** Hump bridge. **Figure 10:** Loose chippings on the road. **Figure 11:** Risk of grounding. **Figure 27:** Tunnel ahead [at distance shown] **Figure 28:** Distance over which road humps extend. **Figure 29:** The exclamation mark indicates danger, the plate below the nature of the danger.

7: Figure 6 Road works. **Figure 25** A low bridge or tunnel **Figure 30** a school bus [sign is displayed on front or rear window].

8: A cycle route

Traffic Signals

DIRECTION SIGNS

1: *What shape are most direction signs?*

2: *Where will you find directional signs with backgrounds coloured* **i]**white **ii]** green **iii]** blue, and how many of these sign-types have white borders?

3: *Figure 1, Where are you when you see this sign?*

4: *Figure 2, What is coming up on the left when you see this sign? And Figure 3,where does this sign come in relation to Figure 2?*

5: *Figure 4, The downward pointing arrows on this motorway sign mean... What?*

6: **Figure 5,** *Fill in the gaps in this resumé of all the information on this motorway sign. There is a deliberate mistake. Can you spot it? And which motorway are you driving on?*

Coventry East and **i]**.......can be reached by leaving the motorway at the next junction, that is Junction **ii]**....... which is **iii]**....... miles further on. You will then be on the M69. If continuing on the motorway you are heading in the general direction of **iv]**....... England, with Birmingham and .... **v]**.......along the route.

7: Figure 6, Figure 8 and **Figure 9,** [A46 Lincoln 12...] are signs relevant to junctions. As you drive along the road in which order will you see them? *[Ignore the fact that the signs shown are not guides to the same places]*

8: *Figure 7, How do you signal on this roundabout if you intend to go to St. Albans?*

9:Figure 10, [Gatwick]. If you follow this sign, which triangular warning sign can you expect to see about two miles on?

10: *Figure 11, Does this sign indicate* **i]** a roundabout **ii]** roadworks **iii]** a ring road **iv]** route closed **v]** rough road surface?

NON-PRIMARY ROUTES

11: Figure 12, *From the information on this sign, describe the layout of the junction ahead.*

12: Figure 13, *If you turn onto the B6049 after seeing this sign, what problem could you encounter before you get to Bradwell?*

13: Figure 14, *This sign can be found* **i]** after a junction **ii]** before it **iii]** at a junction?

14: Figure 15 *What does the symbol on the right indicate on this toilet direction sign?*

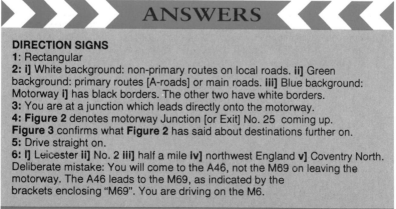

>>> **ANSWERS** <<<

DIRECTION SIGNS

1: Rectangular

2: i] White background: non-primary routes on local roads. **ii]** Green background: primary routes [A-roads] or main roads. **iii]** Blue background: Motorway **i]** has black borders. The other two have white borders.

3: You are at a junction which leads directly onto the motorway.

4: Figure 2 denotes motorway Junction [or Exit] No. 25 coming up. **Figure 3** confirms what **Figure 2** has said about destinations further on.

5: Drive straight on.

6: I] Leicester **ii]** No. 2 **iii]** half a mile **iv]** northwest England **v]** Coventry North. Deliberate mistake: You will come to the A46, not the M69 on leaving the motorway. The A46 leads to the M69, as indicated by the brackets enclosing "M69". You are driving on the M6.

Traffic Signals

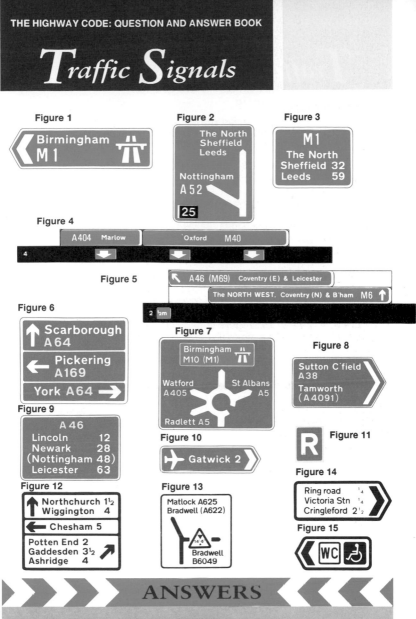

Figure 1
Birmingham
M1

Figure 2
The North
Sheffield
Leeds

Nottingham
A52

25

Figure 3
M1
The North
Sheffield 32
Leeds 59

Figure 4
A404 Marlow | Oxford M40

4

Figure 5
A46 (M69) Coventry (E) & Leicester
The NORTH WEST, Coventry (N) & B'ham M6

2 ½m

Figure 6
Scarborough
A64
Pickering
A169
York A64

Figure 7
Birmingham
M10 (M1)
Watford
A405
St Albans
A5
Radlett A5

Figure 8
Sutton C'field
A38
Tamworth
(A4091)

Figure 9
A46
Lincoln 12
Newark 28
(Nottingham 48)
Leicester 63

Figure 10
Gatwick 2

Figure 11
R

Figure 12
Northchurch 1½
Wiggington 4
Chesham 5
Potten End 2
Gaddesden 3½
Ashridge 4

Figure 13
Matlock A625
Bradwell (A622)
14'6
Bradwell
B6049

Figure 14
Ring road ¼
Victoria Stn ¼
Cringleford 2½

Figure 15
WC

ANSWERS

PRIMARY ROUTES - GREEN BACKGROUND SIGNS
7: Figure 6 is the sort of sign you will see at the approach to a junction. **Figure 8** will be sited AT the junction. **Figure 9** comes after the junction and confirms information on the first sign **Figure 6** about the places which lie ahead.
8: Signal right on entering the roundabout. Continue signalling right until you have passed the third exit [to Birmingham] then signal left for the St. Albans direction.
9: Sign warning of low-flying aircraft or sudden aircraft noise.
10: iii] a ring road
NON-PRIMARY ROUTES
11: The road to Chesham lies at right angles to the road on which you are driving, while the road to Potten End, Gaddesden and Ashridge slants off in a northeasterly direction.
12: Vehicle height restriction: no vehicle over 14.5 feet high may use this road.
13: iii]
14: The stylised figure in a wheelchair is the disabed symbol. It indicates that the toilets have access for disabled persons.

Traffic Signals

OTHER DIRECTION SIGNS

1: *Figure 1* This directional sign has a symbol, on the left, denoting the significance of Wrest Park. What is it?

2: *Figures 1, 2, 3, 4 , and 20* Road signs with brown backgrounds indicate what type of site?

3: *Figures 5, 8 and 9* All these are emergency signs: **TRUE or FALSE?**

4: *Figures 7 and 10* These signs advise routes for pedestrians **[7]** and cyclists **[10]**. Which road users are receiving advice from **Figure 6** and what sort of advice is it?

INFORMATION SIGNS

5: *Figures 11, 16 ,19 and 23* These are signs found in what sort of road?

6: *Figures 17, 24 and 25* What motoring activity is connected with these signs?

7: *Figures 14 , 22 and 26* What does the "T" indicate on these signs?

8: *Figures 12 and 13* These signs denote One Way Streets. **TRUE or FALSE?**

9: *[Figures 15]* Where are the hospital *[Figures 27]* and bus lane?

ANSWERS

OTHER DIRECTION SIGNS

1: Wrest Park or any other site carrying this symbol is an ancient monument cared for by English Heritage.

2: Road signs with brown backgrounds indicate sites of public interest, or offering public facilities.

3: 8] [diversion route] and **9]** [emergency diversion for motorway traffic] are emergency signs. **5]** Indicates a holiday route

4: Lorry drivers. The road numbers A33 and M3 are advised as a suitable route for them.

Traffic Signals

Figure 1

Wrest Park

Figure 2

300yds

Figure 3

300yds

Figure 4

Zoo

Figure 5

HR

Figure 6

(A33,M3)

Figure 7

Council Offices
Public Library

Figure 8

Northtown

Figure 9

Figure 10

Marton 3

Figure 11

M23

Figure 12

ONE WAY

Figure 13

Figure 14

Figure 15

H
Hospital

Figure 16

Figure 17

P

Figure 20   **Figure 18**

Tourist information

Weight limit
10 tonnes
3 miles
ahead

Figure 19

GOOD FOOD
Puddleworth
Services ½ m
Petrol 48.5p

Figure 21

Figure 22

Figure 23

Figure 24

Meter
ZONE
Mon-Fri
8·30am-6·30pm
Saturday
8·30am-1·30pm

Figure 25

Zone
ENDS

Figure 26

Figure 27

Bus lane

ANSWERS

INFORMATION SIGNS

5: A motorway, i.e. Start of the motorway **[11]** End of the motorway **[16]** motorway service area **[19]** Markers for number of yards to junction **[23]**.

6: Parking

7: No through road or lane closed. **22]** also indicates appropriate lanes at junction ahead. **26]** Shows two lanes open, indicated by the arrows.

8: FALSE. Figure 13 tells drivers that vehicles in the left hand lane have priority over those coming from the opposite direction. **Figure 12** is the One Way Street sign.

9: The hospital and bus lane lie ahead. The bus lane is at a junction ahead.

 Road Markings

ROAD MARKINGS

1: **Figures 4 and 5:** Which of these **STOP**
marking signs tells you to stop at signals or a
police control point?

2: **Figures 1, 2 and 3:** Which of these markings
can be found at a roundabout?

ALONG THE CARRIAGEWAY

3: **Figure 6:** When these double white lines are
on your right as you drive, which of them are you
permitted to cross in order to overtake?

4: **Figure 7:** These white diagonal stripes painted
on the road are there to separate traffic or
protect traffic turning right. What other form may
such markings take?

5: **Figure 8:** Which of these three-lane markings
indicates the centre of the road?

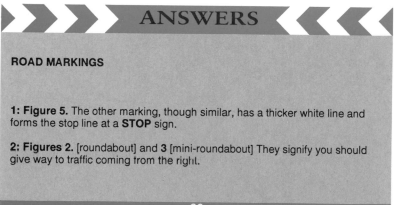

>>> ANSWERS <<<

ROAD MARKINGS

1: Figure 5. The other marking, though similar, has a thicker white line and forms the stop line at a **STOP** sign.

2: Figures 2. [roundabout] and **3** [mini-roundabout] They signify you should give way to traffic coming from the right.

*R*oad *M*arkings

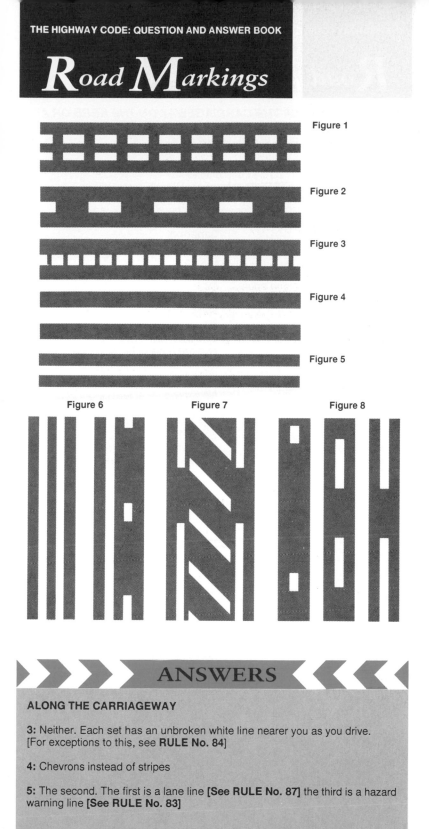

Figure 1

Figure 2

Figure 3

Figure 4

Figure 5

Figure 6   Figure 7   Figure 8

ANSWERS

ALONG THE CARRIAGEWAY

3: Neither. Each set has an unbroken white line nearer you as you drive. [For exceptions to this, see **RULE No. 84**]

4: Chevrons instead of stripes

5: The second. The first is a lane line **[See RULE No. 87]** the third is a hazard warning line **[See RULE No. 83]**

*R*oad *M*arkings

ALONG THE EDGE OF THE CARRIAGEWAY/ON THE KERB OR AT THE EDGE OF THE CARRIAGEWAY

1: *Yellow lines at the edges of roads come in two forms*
i] close to the gutter and
ii] across the kerb. Which type denotes restrictions on waiting, which on parking and which on loading and unloading?

2: Plate: "At any time" and **Plate** "Mon-Sat": What is restricted or forbidden by these plates?

3: The captions to these yellow line markings have been mixed up. **Sort them out:**

Markings	Captions
i] Single yellow line along edge of road	*No waiting in any other period not already covered by the other two edge-of-the-road markings* **[a]**
ii] Double yellow lines along edge of road	*No loading. Monday to Friday 8.00 a.m. and 9.30 a.m. or 4.30 pm and 6.30 p.m.* **[b]**
iii] Broken yellow line along edge of road	*No waiting for at least eight hours between 7 a.m. and 7 p.m. on tour or more days of the week* **[c]**
iv] Two yellow lines across the kerb	*No loading at anytime on any working day* **[d]**
v] Three yellow lines across the kerb	*No waiting for at least eight hours between 7 a m. and 7 p.m. plus additional period outside these times* **[e]**
vi] One yellow line across the kerb	*No loading Monday to Saturday between 8.30 a.m. and 6.30 p.m.* **[f]**

4: How does the first plate differ from the other three?

| Mon - Sat 8am - 6pm Waiting limited to 20 minutes Return prohibited within 40 minutes | No loading Mon-Sat 8·30 am - 6·30 pm | No loading at any time | No loading Mon-Fri 8·00-9·30 am 4·30-6·30 pm |

> **ANSWERS**

ALONG THE EDGE OF THE CARRIAGEWAY/ON THE KERB OR AT THE EDGE OF THE CARRIAGEWAY

1: Yellow lines close to the gutter denote restrictions on waiting. Yellow lines across the kerb denote restrictions on loading and unloading. Restrictions on parking are, by inference, included in restrictions on waiting.

2: Waiting. Plate "At any Time" forbids waiting at all times; Plate "Mon-Sat" limits waiting to times or days outside those shown on the plate.

Road Markings

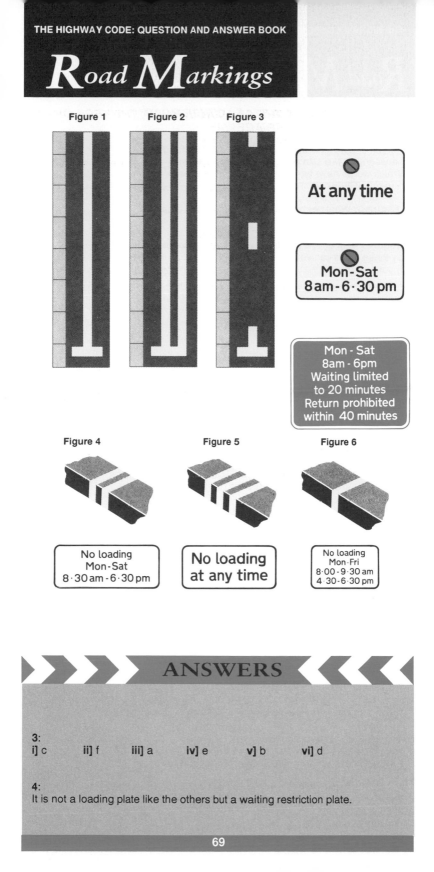

Figure 1 **Figure 2** **Figure 3**

🚫
At any time

🚫
**Mon-Sat
8am-6.30 pm**

Mon - Sat
8am - 6pm
Waiting limited
to 20 minutes
Return prohibited
within 40 minutes

Figure 4 **Figure 5** **Figure 6**

No loading
Mon-Sat
8.30 am-6.30 pm

No loading
at any time

No loading
Mon-Fri
8.00-9.30 am
4.30-6.30 pm

ANSWERS

3:

i] c   **ii]** f   **iii]** a   **iv]** e   **v]** b   **vi]** d

4:
It is not a loading plate like the others but a waiting restriction plate.

Road Markings & Signs

ZEBRA CONTROLLED AREAS / OTHER ROAD MARKINGS

1: Which crossings could you find inside the rectangle between the two sets of zig-zag lines? **[Figure 1]** Which words have been deleted before and after "keep"? **[Figure 2]**

2: Figure 3: What lies ahead when you see this sign and where do you see it?

3: Figures 4, 5, 6, 7, 8 and **9** On which areas marked by these signs can you
i] park **ii]** drive ?

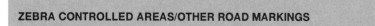

ANSWERS

ZEBRA CONTROLLED AREAS/OTHER ROAD MARKINGS

1: Figure 1: Zebra, Pelican or Puffin pedestrian crossings.
Figure 2: The message reads **"SCHOOL keep CLEAR"**. Vehicles must not park or wait here, not even to set down or pick up schoolchildren.

2: There is a **GIVE WAY** signal ahead. The triangle is painted on the road approaching the signal.

Road Markings & Signs

Figure 1

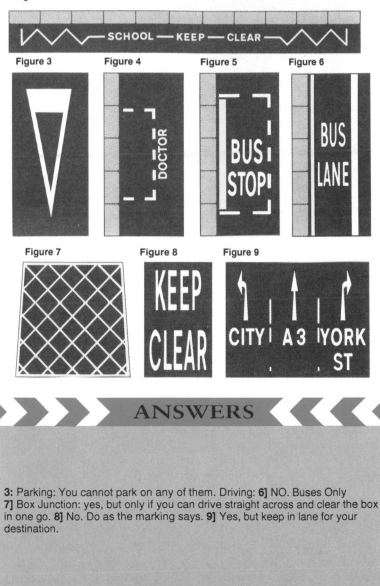

Figure 2

Figure 3 **Figure 4** **Figure 5** **Figure 6**

Figure 7 **Figure 8** **Figure 9**

►►► ANSWERS ◄◄◄

3: Parking: You cannot park on any of them. Driving: **6]** NO. Buses Only
7] Box Junction: yes, but only if you can drive straight across and clear the box in one go. **8]** No. Do as the marking says. **9]** Yes, but keep in lane for your destination.

Vehicle Markings

VEHICLE MARKINGS

1: *Where will you see striped red and yellow markings while driving along the road?*

i] on builders' skips placed on the pavement **ii]** at road works
iii] at a hazard in the road, for instance a flood caused by an overflowing drain? **iv]** on commercial vehicles 12 meters long?
v] at failed traffic lights?

HAZARD WARNING PLATES

2: *This is a plate with hazard warning of the kind you will see on tank vehicles carrying dangerous goods, in this case Flammable Liquid. If the flame symbol remains the same, but the top half of the diamond-shaped hazard warning symbol were white and the lower half red, what would the warning message read?*

3: *What colour is the diamond hazard warning-plate for "Oxidizing Substance" and which of these symbols will you see on it?*
i] RADIO ACTIVE. **ii]** CORROSIVE. **iii]** OXIDIZING AGENT.
iv] TOXIC SUBSTANCE.

4: Match up these colours, symbols and warning messages to make the correct plates. Which colour plate is not a diamond shape?

Diamond shape coloured:	Symbol for	Message
1] Plain white	i]Multi loads	a] Toxic substance
2] White top, black bottom half	ii] Non-flammable compressed gas	b] Corrosive substance
3] White top, red bottom half	iii] Toxic substance	c] Multi loads
4] Dark Green	iv] Corrosive substance	d] Radio Active
5] Orange	v] Radio active substance	e] Non-flammable compressed gas
6] Yellow	vi] Spontaneously combustible substance	f] Spontaneously combustible substance
	vii] Oxidizing agent substance	g] Oxidizing substance

PROJECTION MARKERS

5: *These markers are carried as warning signs on loads which project more than two meters from the front or rear of a vehicle. Which is carried at the side and which at the end [viz. front or back] ?*

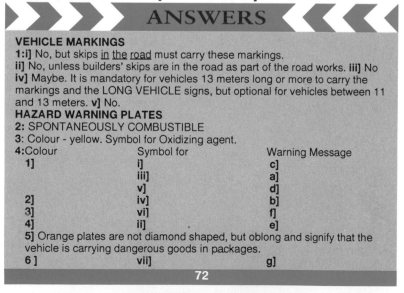

ANSWERS

VEHICLE MARKINGS

1:i] No, but skips in the road must carry these markings.
ii] No, unless builders' skips are in the road as part of the road works. **iii]** No **iv]** Maybe. It is mandatory for vehicles 13 meters long or more to carry the markings and the LONG VEHICLE signs, but optional for vehicles between 11 and 13 meters. **v]** No.

HAZARD WARNING PLATES

2: SPONTANEOUSLY COMBUSTIBLE
3: Colour - yellow. Symbol for Oxidizing agent.

4:Colour	Symbol for	Warning Message
1]	i]	c]
	iii]	a]
	v]	d]
2]	iv]	b]
3]	vi]	f]
4]	ii]	e]

5] Orange plates are not diamond shaped, but oblong and signify that the vehicle is carrying dangerous goods in packages.

| **6]** | vii] | g] |

*V*ehicle *M*arkings

VEHICLE MARKINGS

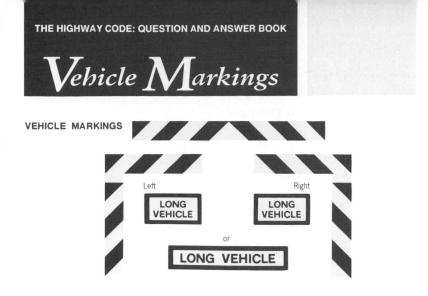

HAZARD WARNING PLATES

The above panel will be displayed by vehicles carrying certain dangerous goods in packages

PROJECTION MARKERS

ANSWERS

5: Large right-angled triangle: at the side of the vehicle. Small inverted triangle.

The Law

THE ROAD USER AND THE LAW

1 *As a driver, which documents do you have to possess and if necessary, display or produce at the request of the police?*

2: *What do you do if your documents are not immediately available when requested by the police?*

3: *What is the minimum continuous tread depth car tyres are required to have by law across the centre threequarters of their width?*
At least
i] 2 mm
ii] 1 mm
iii] 1.6 mm
iv] 1.8 mm

4: *Do passengers sitting in*
i] the front of the car
ii] the back of the car-have to wear seat belts?

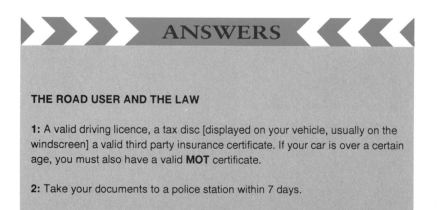

ANSWERS

THE ROAD USER AND THE LAW

1: A valid driving licence, a tax disc [displayed on your vehicle, usually on the windscreen] a valid third party insurance certificate. If your car is over a certain age, you must also have a valid **MOT** certificate.

2: Take your documents to a police station within 7 days.

The Law

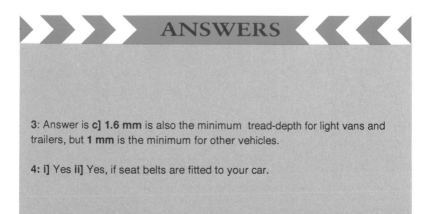

ANSWERS

3: Answer is **c]** **1.6 mm** is also the minimum tread-depth for light vans and trailers, but **1 mm** is the minimum for other vehicles.

4: i] Yes ii] Yes, if seat belts are fitted to your car.

The Law

PENALTIES

1: *What are penalty points and who imposes them?*

2: *If a driver accumulates 14 penalty points in three years how long can s/he be disqualified from driving as a result?*

3: *Could the Driver and Vehicle Licensing Agency's Medical Branch suspect a driver of having an alcohol problem if:*

i] the driver has been convicted of drinking and driving twice in
  a] 12 years
  b] 10 years.
ii] the driver has been convicted once in ten years while
  a] two times over the legal limit
  b] three times over the legal limit

4: *Can a driver refuse to give a specimen if asked by the police?*

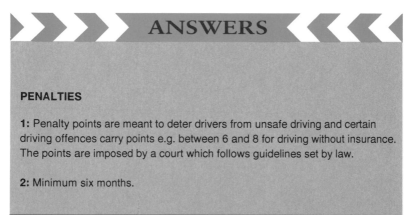

ANSWERS

PENALTIES

1: Penalty points are meant to deter drivers from unsafe driving and certain driving offences carry points e.g. between 6 and 8 for driving without insurance. The points are imposed by a court which follows guidelines set by law.

2: Minimum six months.

The Law

>>> **ANSWERS** <<<

3: i]a] No. **i]b]** Yes **ii]a]** No   **ii]b]** Yes [two and one half times over the legal limit is the minimum amount for which drivers will come under suspicion.

4: A driver can refuse, but as a result will be suspected of having an alcohol problem.

The Law

PENALTY TABLE

1: *Which of these three offences is considered the most serious as shown by the maximum penalties each can incur?*
i] Causing death through careless driving under the influence of drink
ii] Causing death by dangerous driving
iii] Causing death through careless driving under the influence of drugs

2: *Can a driver be imprisoned for the following offences? If so, for how long?*
i] Driving while unfit through drink or drugs
ii] Failing to provide a specimen for analysis
iii] Driving after a licence has been refused or revoked because of medical considerations?
iv] Failing to stop after an accident
v] Failing to report an accident
vi] Driving while disqualified
vii] Speeding
vii] Driving without insurance

3: *What is the maximum fine which courts can impose for driving offences generally?*

4: *What penalty points can accrue if a driver is convicted of:*
i] careless driving
ii] inconsiderate driving
iii] driving while disqualified.
iv] Not having an **MOT** certificate ??

5: *A driver convicted of dangerous driving may receive 2 years' imprisonment. What other penalties could this offence incur?*

6: *For which of the following offences*
i] **MUST** courts disqualfy a driver, and for which
ii] do courts have discretion to disqualify if thought *advisable?*

a] Careless and inconsiderate driving   b] Driving while disqualified
c] Driving while unfit through drink or drugs. d] Driving while over the legal alcohol limit   e] Failing to identify the driver of a vehicle   f] Speeding
g] Refusing to provide a specimen for analysis.

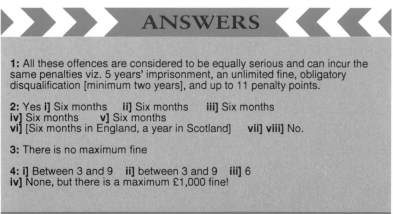

►►► ANSWERS ◄◄◄

1: All these offences are considered to be equally serious and can incur the same penalties viz. 5 years' imprisonment, an unlimited fine, obligatory disqualification [minimum two years], and up to 11 penalty points.

2: Yes i] Six months   ii] Six months   iii] Six months
iv] Six months   v] Six months
vi] [Six months in England, a year in Scotland]   vii] viii] No.

3: There is no maximum fine

4: i] Between 3 and 9   ii] between 3 and 9   iii] 6
iv] None, but there is a maximum £1,000 fine!

The Law

7: *How much can a driver be fined for*
i] Not wearing a seat belt
ii] Driving without insurance
iii] Traffic light offences, such as driving through a red light
iv] Speeding on the motorway
v] Driving while disqualified in Scotland.

8: *Driving otherwise than in accordance with the provisions of a licence can attract a fine of £1,000. Can a cyclist be fined more, less or the same for*
i] dangerous cycling
ii] careless cycling ?

9: *For which of these offences can a driver receive more than five penalty points?*
i] Driving while unfit through drugs or drink   **ii]** Driving with excess alcohol
iii] Failing to provide a specimen for analysis
iv] Failing to stop after an accident   **v]** Failing to report an accident
vi] Driving after a licence has been refused or revoked on medical grounds.
vii] Driving without insurance

10: *What fines can be imposed for the following offences?*
i] Careless and inconsiderate driving
ii] Driving while unfit through drink or drugs
iii] Failing to stop after an accident
iv] Driving after a licence has been refused or revoked on medical grounds
v] Failing to identify the driver of a vehicle.

11: *For which of these offences can the court order the driver to take a fresh, and extended test?*
i] Dangerous driving
ii] Speeding
iii] Careless or inconsiderate driving ?

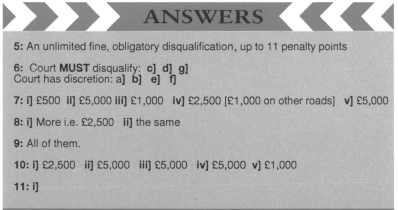

ANSWERS

5: An unlimited fine, obligatory disqualification, up to 11 penalty points

6: Court **MUST** disqualify: **c] d] g]**
Court has discretion: **a] b] e] f]**

7: i] £500 **ii]** £5,000 **iii]** £1,000 **iv]** £2,500 [£1,000 on other roads] **v]** £5,000

8: i] More i.e. £2,500 **ii]** the same

9: All of them.

10: i] £2,500 **ii]** £5,000 **iii]** £5,000 **iv]** £5,000 **v]** £1,000

11: i]

The Law

VEHICLE SECURITY

1: *Apart from the extra expense in getting around and the loss of your possessions, what consequences may the theft of your car have in connection with your insurance?*

2: *As a security device, where on your car could you have your registration number etched?*

3: *When you leave your car, should you take its contents with you or lock them in the boot?*

4: *Checklist for leaving your car - but what is incorrect procedure? Engage the steering lock. Take the ignition key with you. Lock the car. Leave your dog in the car for extra security and close the windows. Hide your vehicle documents in the glove compartment. Take the vehicle's contents with you.*

5: *Which is better for extra security*

i] an anti-theft device
ii] an immobiliser
iii] a car alarm ?

ANSWERS

VEHICLE SECURITY

1: Sorting out the insurance situation with a stolen car could take weeks, and your no claims bonus could be affected.

2: On the windows.

3: Either will suffice

The Law

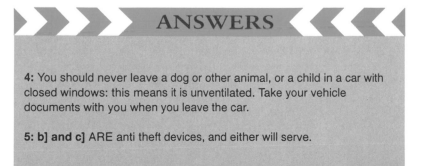

ANSWERS

4: You should never leave a dog or other animal, or a child in a car with closed windows: this means it is unventilated. Take your vehicle documents with you when you leave the car.

5: b] and c] ARE anti theft devices, and either will serve.

Score Chart

Page Number	Number of right answers		
	1st try	2nd try	3rd try
4			
5			
6			
7			
8			
9			
10			
11			
12			
13			
14			
15			
16			
17			
18			
19			
20			
21			
22			
23			
24			
25			
26			
27			
28			
29			
30			
31			
32			
33			
34			
35			
36			
37			
38			
39			
40			
41			
42			

NOTES

Page Number	Number of right answers		
	1st try	2nd try	3rd try
43			
44			
45			
46			
47			
48			
49			
50			
51			
52			
53			
54			
55			
56			
57			
58			
59			
60			
61			
62			
63			
64			
65			
66			
67			
68			
69			
70			
71			
72			
73			
74			
75			
76			
77			
78			
79			
80			
81			
TOTAL:			

Score Chart

Page Number	Number of right answers			Page Number	Number of right answers		
	4th try	6th try	7th try		4th try	5th try	6th try
4				43			
5				44			
6				45			
7				46			
8				47			
9				48			
10				49			
11				50			
12				51			
13				52			
14				53			
15				54			
16				55			
17				56			
18				57			
19				58			
20				59			
21				60			
22				61			
23				62			
24				63			
25				64			
26				65			
27				66			
28				67			
29				68			
30				69			
31				70			
32				71			
33				72			
34				73			
35				74			
36				75			
37				76			
38				77			
39				78			
40				79			
41				80			
42				81			
NOTES				TOTAL:			

Score Chart

Page Number	Number of right answers		
	7th try	8th try	9th try
4			
5			
6			
7			
8			
9			
10			
11			
12			
13			
14			
15			
16			
17			
18			
19			
20			
21			
22			
23			
24			
25			
26			
27			
28			
29			
30			
31			
32			
33			
34			
35			
36			
37			
38			
39			
40			
41			
42			

NOTES

Page Number	Number of right answers		
	7st try	8th try	9th try
43			
44			
45			
46			
47			
48			
49			
50			
51			
52			
53			
54			
55			
56			
57			
58			
59			
60			
61			
62			
63			
64			
65			
66			
67			
68			
69			
70			
71			
72			
73			
74			
75			
76			
77			
78			
79			
80			
81			
TOTAL:			